P9-BHR-558

THE MASS IN THE WEST

IS VOLUME

111

OF THE

Twentieth Century Encyclopedia of Catholicism

UNDER SECTION

X

THE WORSHIP OF THE CHURCH

IT IS ALSO THE

82ND

VOLUME IN ORDER OF PUBLICATION

Edited by HENRI DANIEL-ROPS of the Académie Française

THE MASS IN THE WEST

By *LANCELOT C. SHEPPARD*

HAWTHORN BOOKS · PUBLISHERS · *New York*

First Edition, January, 1962

NIHIL OBSTAT

Hubertus Richards, S.T.L., L.S.S.

Censor Deputatus

IMPRIMATUR

E. Morrogh Bernard

Vicarius Generalis

Westmonasterii, die XXIII Decembris, MCMLXI

CONTENTS

INTRODUCTION

It is beginning to be seen with increasing clarity that if we are to understand the Roman rite properly we must know something of its origins, history and evolution; this is the task of *ressourcement* (an untranslatable but expressive word). *The History of the Mass* by F. Amiot and *The Eastern Liturgies* by I. H. Dalmais (both in this series) provide some of this necessary information. The present short volume is intended to fill in some of the gaps by offering an account of those variants of the Roman rite still in use today. To avoid so far as possible monotonous repetition they have not all been described on the same pattern. A fairly full account has been given of the Ambrosian and Mozarabic rites because the first is important as an example of Roman liturgical development at a certain stage, and the second, though now almost defunct, shows us the shape, though a little deformed, of the liturgy in Europe north of the Alps and in Spain before the imposition of the Roman rite by Charlemagne. The liturgy of Lyons is described more summarily because it is far nearer the modern Roman rite; similarly, the rite of Braga, confined to one diocese in Portugal, because of its affinities and great similarity with the Roman rite is also accorded summary treatment. There is a type of liturgical writing, over-concerned with details, that will tell us, for example, that at Braga only the celebrant is allowed to wear a biretta at high Mass but omits to show the relationship of one part of the rite to another. I have tried to avoid this.

Again, the Cistercian rite has been given fuller treatment than that of the Carmelites, for example, because, despite the fact that it is only just now being revived according to its original form, it provides an excellent example of the development of a variant rite in the West and much of the information here given is not easily available in English. And the early history of the rite forms the necessary groundwork for the study of the Premonstratensian and Dominican rites.

Finally, a note about the principle followed in giving, or not giving, the Latin text or translation of versicles, prayers, etc. The parts of the Roman *Ordo Missae* are referred to by the Latin words with which they begin. Thus, the embolism after the Lord's Prayer is called the *Libera,* the commemoration of the saints after the memento of the dead is referred to as the *Nobis quoque peccatoribus.* In other words, familiarity with the order of Mass in the modern Roman Missal is assumed. When a prayer of some length from another rite is quoted the cue is given in Latin so that it can be identified in other books on the subject, but the whole prayer or part of it is given in English when it is thought necessary to quote it to show the particular emphasis implied or to illustrate a point. These translations, unless otherwise stated, are the author's. Versicles, responses and short Latin phrases are translated as often as thought necessary immediately after the Latin version. Familiar versicles from the Roman rite are not translated. In this way it is hoped that those who know little or no Latin will not be at a disadvantage.

PLAN OF THIS BOOK

After an introductory chapter on the evolution of the Roman liturgy, Chapter II considers the rites of Milan (Ambrosian) and Toledo (Mozarabic). After a note on origins and history, the rite of Mass, as it is actually in use, is described and outstanding peculiarities are mentioned. Chapter III is concerned in the same way with two other diocesan rites, those of Lyons and Braga. Chapter IV is devoted to the rites of the monastic Orders (Carthusians, Cistercians, Carmelites, Dominicans and Premonstratensians). Three appendices (on the neo-Gallican rites, the Sarum rite and the Glagolitic or Roman-Slavonic liturgy) conclude the book.

CHAPTER I

THE ROMAN RITE AND ITS VARIANTS

The title page of the Missal in use in the Church today wherever the Roman rite is followed shows clearly the origin of the book: *Missale Romanum ex decreto sacrosancti Concilii Tridentini restitutum S. Pii V Pontificis Maximi Jussu editum.* . . : "The Roman Missal, restored by decree of the sacred Council of Trent and published by order of St Pius V, supreme Pontiff. . ." It is, then, the Missal of the Church of the Council of Trent, restored as an affirmation of the unity of doctrine within the Church and for the purpose of putting an end to a period of liturgical chaos that had developed with increasing momentum in the course of upwards of six hundred years. Times of crisis very often produce remedies that betray their origins only too clearly and if that danger was not wholly avoided in the sixteenth-century liturgical reform it is nevertheless cause for thankfulness that what emerged from the reforming commission's labours on the whole preserved rather than destroyed, added rather than deleted, many features with which we are familiar in the modern Mass of the Roman Missal.[1]

[1] For the history of the various parts of the Mass reference can be made to the volume on the subject in this series: F. Amiot, *History of the Mass.* The present volume avoids so far as possible many matters, more especially the history of various elements of the ordinary of the Mass, that are dealt with in detail in Amiot's book.

Possibly the most revealing word on the title page of the Missal is the word *Romanum*. It informs us that the book contains the liturgy of the local Roman Church, and that in Great Britain, for example, or in Ireland, in the U.S.A. and as far afield as China or Australia, the rite of Mass is that of Rome for all Catholics who owe obedience to the pope not only as supreme Pontiff of the Universal Church but as Patriarch of the West. The other rites of Christendom are, equally with the Roman rite, fully authentic expressions of Catholic worship and, for those who belong to them, are obligatory in the same way that the Roman rite is of obligation for most western Catholics.

"Rite follows patriarchate", and, though this is basically true, it is probably equally true to say that no other rite besides the Roman reflects so faithfully the local practice of the mother Church. The calendar has developed around the names of the early Roman martyrs, the first saints to find a place in the liturgy; the saints mentioned in the canon of the Mass are those celebrated in Rome in the early Church; lastly, many of the Masses of the season bear at their head a topographical note with reference to a church in Rome. Thus on the Saturday after the third Sunday of Lent we find *Statio ad S. Susannam*, "Station at St Susanna's [church]", the church, namely, to which the pope, clergy and people of Rome went in procession and there offered Mass. Examination of the proper of this Mass reveals that the Scripture passages have been chosen in connection with the church in question. And there are many other details of the same sort scattered throughout the Missal; they are clear evidence of the fact that essentially the rite of the Roman Mass is that of the city of Rome. In the proper sense of the term, therefore, those who follow this rite are Roman Catholics in the same way that Catholics who follow another rite are entitled to call themselves Catholics of that rite.

Rite follows patriarchate, but this must not be taken to

mean that there is no room whatever for local variations within the same rite. Local customs grow up and are tolerated, men differ from country to country, from race to race, and it is obvious that some small variations will be found from place to place; nevertheless, wherever the Roman rite is of obligation the liturgical books and the Mass formularies are the same.[2] To this principle of liturgical practice there is however one important exception.

VARIANTS OF THE ROMAN RITE

It is often said that the Council of Trent ushered in a period of rigid liturgical uniformity in the West and that the ensuing few centuries saw the halt of all liturgical development as a result of which there began a period of fossilization and rubricism whose end we are only just beginning to see with the recent reforms in the Roman rite. There is certainly much truth in this assertion; it was part of the price paid for the essential remedy provided at a period that sorely needed it. Yet the Bull (*Quo primum tempore*) of St Pius V authorizing the new Roman Missal (July 9th, 1570), although it laid down categorically enough that throughout the Church in the West it was most fitting (*maxime deceat*) that there should be but one rite of celebrating Mass (*unum Missae celebrandae ritum*), it nevertheless allowed that those local Churches and religious Orders whose rites could show a prescription of at least two hundred years should be permitted to keep them, although they could, should they wish, adopt the new Roman Missal. Many hastened to do so; others reformed their own books in accordance with the principles of the new ₊Roman reform; other rites, for a variety of reasons, quietly dis-

[2] The reference here is to the *Ordo Missae,* usually known as the Ordinary of the Mass; on certain days there are of course variations in the Proper (or variable) parts of the Mass due to the celebration of local feasts and local changes in the general calendar. See the volume in this series, *The Christian Calendar.*

appeared. The religious upheaval in England in the sixteenth century, for example, in spite of the short period of revival under Mary Tudor, caused the disappearance of the local English variants which, had things turned out differently, might well have survived until our own times.[3]

Certain other rites survived elsewhere in Europe until the nineteenth century, but merely as interesting survivals of another age. Liturgy is a living thing, the expression of man's public worship of God in its highest form, and there can hardly be more than archaeological regret that so many of these relics of a past age and a very different climate of liturgical practice have disappeared. To attempt to revive them now would be absurd.[4]

There were some rites, however, with a sufficiently strong following for them to remain the living expression of a traditional way of worship which enabled them to continue in use down to the present. It is the purpose of this book to give the principal facts of their history and origins and to describe their chief characteristics.

COMPARATIVE LITURGY

"The comparative study of the languages of a single group enables us to describe the laws governing their evolution and to reconstruct the primitive system from which they

[3] The Sarum rite (that of the diocese of Salisbury in England which was the most widespread) was used in secret by some few Marian priests at the beginning of the reign of Elizabeth but the first missionaries from the Continent brought with them, it is said, the newly reformed Missal of St Pius V. Research needs to be done on this question; not only the service books but discipline in such matters as fasting and abstinence differed between rite and rite, Salisbury and Rome; how long did the Sarum fasting rules survive in England? In England and Wales the marriage service in use has certain Sarum peculiarities not to be found in the jejune formulary of the Roman Ritual. See Appendix II.

[4] As Cardinal Vaughan well understood when it was proposed at the foundation of Westminster Cathedral to restore the Sarum rite for use in the daily liturgy. Wisely he refrained from attempting to do so.

derive, even when no vestiges of it survive. In the same way, the comparison of the different liturgies enables us to formulate the laws of their evolution and to disengage their primitive elements."[5] These remarks in connection with the comparison of the liturgies of East and West are of almost equal relevance in the sphere of western liturgies; they are also an application of the principle of *ressourcement,* the principle, that is, of the return to origins, very much in vogue at the present time; such a return is important because it represents the only hope of meaningful reform, a reform based on authenticity of rite and gesture which makes liturgy the real action of a worshipping community. The application of this principle does not consist, of course, in looking to the past merely and only for the sake of copying it. Liturgy is continually evolving and it has been doing so for the past two thousand years. We look to the past to formulate the laws of this evolution, for it is only when we have understood these laws that we can usefully make our own contribution at the present time to this evolutionary process.

RITE AND USE

At one time, particularly among English-speaking liturgists, a distinction was made between a *rite* in the sense of a liturgy (for example, the Roman rite) and a *use,* the variant form of a rite used in a certain locality or by certain sections in the Church. Thus, the present liturgy of the Carthusians would be termed a use because it is really derived from the Roman rite and is only a variant of it. There are some advantages in using this terminology but it is apt to lead to confusion. Thus we are led to inquire at the outset whether the Ambrosian liturgy of Milan is a "use" or a "rite"; the question can only be decided on the basis of origins and this is precisely where

[5] Dom Botte, in his Introduction to *Comparative Liturgy* by Anton Baumstark (London, 1958), p. viii. See Select Bibliography at the end of this volume.

difficulties occur because, as we shall see, the origin of the Ambrosian liturgy is the subject of considerable discussion.[6] In this book the term rite is used throughout.

THE ROMAN RITE FROM THE ORIGINS TO TRENT

Since this book deals with the variants of the Roman liturgy it is important to bear in mind that this rite forms but one of the liturgical "families" that have evolved in the course of time.[7] I trace here very rapidly the history of the Roman rite down to the Council of Trent in the sixteenth century in order to provide the framework within which to place the history and development of the various liturgies with which we are here concerned.

Origins

From the Eucharist in the New Testament down to the *Didache* (or *Doctrine of the Apostles*) in the first half of the second century or Justin Martyr's account (*c.* A.D. 150) we can see that a certain evolution has taken place. Earlier than this (*c.* A.D. 112) Pliny the Younger having arrested and examined a number of Christians tells us that they were accustomed to meet together on a certain fixed day before the dawn and sing together a hymn to Christ as God, that they bound themselves by oath not to do wrong and then dispersed. They gathered together again at a later hour for a harmless meal.[8]

[6] That in this particular case the term leads to confusion can be seen in the *Oxford Dictionary of the Christian Church* (Oxford University Press, 2nd edn, 1958), a usually reliable work of reference, in which the Ambrosian liturgy is termed a rite on p. 42 and a use on p. 1400.

[7] A conspectus of the liturgical families of the East will be found in I.-H. Dalmais, O.P., *The Eastern Liturgies*, translated by Donald Attwater, in this series.

[8] A translation of Pliny's letter will be found in B. J. Kidd, *Documents Illustrative of Church History*. Justin's account is reprinted in this series in Amiot, *op. cit.*, p. 13.

In Justin we see that the eucharistic service contained two well-defined elements: prayers, reading and a homily, forming the first part of the service which was followed by the bringing in of the bread and wine, prayer over them and communion by those present. These somewhat slender indications take us up to the beginning of the third century. It is only comparatively recently that an important discovery has enabled us to reconstitute to some extent the practice of the Church at Rome at this time. Not that there was a definite formulary at this early date but that there can be discerned an established framework within which the celebrant improvises his part; extempore prayer seems still to be the rule. This discovery was that of the *Apostolic Tradition* of Hippolytus who, at one time an antipope, was later reconciled to the Church and was martyred in 235.[9]

Another document of approximately the same date, at any rate of the first half of the third century, is the *Didascalia*, a Syriac document which was later embodied in the *Apostolic Constitutions* (fourth century). Comparison of Hippolytus and the *Didascalia* shows us, as Jungmann pertinently remarks, that liturgical prayer was still "elastic and continually subject to new influences":

> But at the same time there is a good deal to show that for the general course of the liturgy in the Church as a whole, there was a unified order, a network of still flexible regulations stamped with the authority of custom. These statutes regulated the building of the house of God, the time and manner of

---

[9] Dom R. H. Connolly was responsible for this discovery. See his *The So-called Egyptian Church Order* (Cambridge, 1916). Extracts in translation will be found in Amiot, *op. cit.,* pp. 15 following. As to extempore prayer: "It is not necessary for the bishop to use the exact wording which we gave above, as if he were learning them by heart for his thanksgiving to God. Rather each one should pray according to his capacity...." For the full text see G. Dix's translation (from which the above extract is taken): *The Treatise on the Apostolic Tradition of St Hippolytus* (London, 1937), p. 19.

service, the division of functions, the way prayers were to begin and end, and so forth. The fundamental design of the prayer of thanks—the Eucharist—is everywhere the same: it begins invariably with a short dialogue and closes with the Amen of the people.[10]

It appears clearly that though there was one liturgical pattern which was suitable for all places—it is proved, for example, by Hippolytus' work being in use as far away as Ethiopia—yet there was some concern to make allowances for local conditions, to adopt a phraseology and the rest which, while faithful to original tradition, should be adapted to the needs of the local congregation.

The trend of the local adaptation emerges more clearly towards the end of the fourth century. Whether, as is sometimes asserted, it was Pope Damasus (366–84) who was responsible for the substitution of Latin for Greek as the language for worship at Rome, we cannot be sure. Certainly it was about this time that the change took place; Greek was gradually losing ground as the *lingua franca* of the capital of the Roman Empire and the change was necessary. Yet Latin as a language for worship was no novelty; North Africa had known it before this time and in the North of Italy Milan seems to have preceded Rome in its adoption.

The celebration at Rome of the anniversaries of the martyrs, and the gradual adoption (from the East) of the various feasts commemorating the events in our Lord's life, led to the emergence of what can be termed a liturgical cycle which required for its different occasions a selection of texts suitable for each celebration. Thus gradually were compiled those collections of prayers and Scripture passages which came to be one of the distinguishing marks of the Roman liturgy. This development had occurred certainly by the fifth–sixth centuries; in it can be seen something more than the merely

[10] J. A. Jungmann, S.J., *The Mass of the Roman Rite* (*Missarum Solemnia*), vol. I, p. 32.

embryonic form of our liturgical year with its Mass formularies "proper" to each solemnity.

At the same time the framework of the liturgy, the invariable prayers of the canon primarily, emerge as a fixed form remarkable for their conciseness of phrase and succinctness of expression. The same characteristics are to be found in the collects.[11]

The earliest surviving liturgical book of the Roman rite is the work referred to as the *Leonine Sacramentary*. It is known to us in a single manuscript of the early seventh century belonging to the Chapter library of Verona (*codex 85*) and was first printed in the eighteenth century. Unfortunately, it is incomplete and lacks both the order and canon of Mass, but it contains many Mass propers which still find a place in our Missal. Both its ascription to St Leo (†461) and its designation as a Sacramentary are arbitrary; certain of its prayers however may well have been composed by him. This collection of prayers is in the form of a private collection of booklets (*libelli*) which circulated independently; they seem however to have come originally from the Lateran. From this evidence it seems clear that up to this period there was no one official collection of prayers but several from which a choice was made according to needs and circumstances and to which additions could be made as necessity required.

The Sacramentaries

Of the next period (roughly from the beginning of the seventh century down to the middle of the tenth) in the evolution of the Roman rite we are considerably better informed. The fourteen years of the pontificate of St Gregory the Great (590–604) seem to have been crucial in the development of the Roman liturgy. The state of the rite as he found it at the

[11] A discussion of the various questions concerning the origin and development of the canon of the Roman Mass would be out of place here. Readers will find some information in Amiot, *op. cit.*, pp. 49–60, with the reference there given.

beginning of his pontificate can be established with some accuracy, though also with some gaps, for the form of this liturgy can be seen in the Gelasian Sacramentary which is, in fact, the oldest Roman Massbook in the proper sense of the term. It is undoubtedly not to be ascribed to St Gelasius (he was pope 492–6) but it seems certain that it is no later than the latter half of the sixth century.

St Gregory's work on this material seems, most probably, to have been in the direction of simplification and more orderly arrangement—the reduction of the variable prayers at each Mass to three (collect, secret and postcommunion) and a reduction also of the variations occurring within the canon—prefaces and additional forms for the *Communicantes* and *Hanc igitur*. But St Gregory's principal work was certainly the definitive arrangement of the Roman canon. The lectionary (lessons, Epistles and Gospels) was also settled at this time but this was subjected to considerable change subsequently.

It was this form of the Roman liturgy that gradually spread and became predominant not only in Italy but also beyond the Alps. The prestige of the Roman Church, the sober nature of her liturgy, the fact that at Rome were the tombs of the Princes of the Apostles and many martyrs besides, all combined to give her form of worship a special *cachet* of authenticity and authority. In addition, the absence of any great primatial see in Europe at this period (save in Visigothic Spain) and the troubled nature of the times favoured this rapid expansion.

At the same time in different centres the Roman liturgy absorbed features of other, local traditions which, deriving from an earlier period and possibly with affinities to eastern usages, had not evolved as they had done at Rome.

Modifications and additions

The attempts of Pepin III ("the Short": 714–68) to achieve liturgical uniformity throughout his kingdom by the imposition of the Roman liturgy resulted in the widespread adoption not of the Gregorian recension of the Sacramentary but of a mixture of Gelasian elements with those already prevailing in his realms. Charlemagne (*c.* 742–814), continuing this policy, requested from Rome an authentic copy of the Roman liturgy. He was sent, curiously enough, only a festival book (which did not contain, therefore, the ordinary Sunday Masses) and it was Alcuin who added what was required together with other elements not hitherto forming part of the authentic Roman recension. What is important to note as a consequence of all this is that gradually, on account of the troubled times at Rome in these centuries, the effective liturgical centre moved from Rome to the churches of the Moselle and the Rhine and the great monasteries dotted over the countryside round about them—to St Gall, Reichenau and Metz, and also to Burgundy.

It was thus no longer the pure Roman liturgy but a Romano-Frankish liturgy which was in the ascendant and which, with the reorganization of the Church in Rome in the second half of the tenth century by German emperors and with the help of the reformed Benedictine monasteries, was introduced into Rome itself. This liturgy displayed two characteristics: the Roman formularies (the collects and canon particularly) were sober and restrained, the added (Gallican) elements were florid in expression and exhibited an exuberance which was in direct contrast with those originally sent to Charlemagne.[12]

The later Middle Ages (*thirteenth to sixteenth centuries*)

This final period down to the Council of Trent can be dealt with quite briefly. Its characteristics are, in Rome, that of a

---

[12] For Alcuin's work see Amiot, *op. cit.*, p. 19. Edmund Bishop in his paper "The Genius of the Roman rite" compares two collects in the Missal—that for the dead (*Fidelium Deus omnium Conditor*) and that for all conditions of men (*Omnipotens*), showing clearly the difference of their origins from the fact of their style.

reaction against the prolixity and ceremonial magnificence of the Romano-Frankish liturgy which had come into being for the reasons that we have seen. Elsewhere local Churches, basing their liturgies on the Romano-Frankish forms, codified their local practices, and in codifying them endowed them with a certain legitimacy and authenticity.

Scripta manent. In Rome, under Innocent III, the reaction came to a head in the need for a liturgy that could be used for the Roman curia, more peripatetic in those days than now; for Mass and Office its officials needed portable books which reduced ceremonial requirements to a minimum. The adoption of these books by the newly-founded Franciscan friars caused them to be spread far and wide so that largely they came to be regarded as the authentic Roman liturgy. New tendencies in eucharistic devotion, the elevation of the Host at Mass in the thirteenth century, the increasing rarity of the reception of Communion by the laity, the numerous private Masses consequent on the many foundations of chantries for the dead and the ordination of all choir monks, the generally low state of education among the laity and most of the lower clergy, with the resultant lack of comprehension of the rites that were celebrated in Latin, all combined to produce a changed conception of the liturgy. No longer common worship of the whole congregation in the sense that it was in, say, Rome of the fifth–sixth centuries, it came to be regarded as something performed on behalf of the congregation by the priest, an obligation to be fulfilled, a rite at which presence was necessary on stated occasions to avoid serious sin; men turned elsewhere to satisfy their devotion and to give expression to their religious needs and aspirations. Thus gradually the worship of the Church as it existed in the Roman rite grew into something performed by the priest in the presence of a congregation that at best was composed of individuals occupied in their own private devotions or at the worst was purely passive.

LOCAL LITURGIES AND THE ROMAN RITE

The foregoing very summary sketch of approximately 1500 years of liturgical history has only been given here since it forms the necessary prelude to consideration of the kind of evolution that has been going on in liturgy since the beginning. This process can be characterized very simply as one of adaptation to needs and localities. It seems to be part of the genius of the Roman rite not only to provide for the needs of worshippers in the West but also to absorb and in absorbing to remould elements received from elsewhere. This happened, as we have seen, with the Romano-Frankish liturgy of the ninth–tenth centuries. It happened also right at the beginning when the Roman rite came into existence.

In the following chapters we shall see something of local development in the West. The two rites—the Ambrosian and the Mozarabic—with which we are first concerned, and despite the somewhat uncertain position regarding their origins, can be regarded as liturgical forms which developed at an early date and outside the main stream of Roman liturgical evolution. The other rites, both diocesan and monastic, represent, to some extent, fixations of the Roman rite at certain stages of its development, as it was practised in certain localities where these variants developed. But just as in the ninth–tenth centuries the Roman rite was influenced from a source external to it, so too it exerted influence in its developed form on the other rites which had survived from an earlier period in its evolution, until at the present day all the variants of the Roman rite, despite the divergencies they exhibit, show greater similarities with their parent than they did in past centuries.[13] There have been liturgists who deplored this tendency to increasing "Romanization"; they forgot that these

---

[13] The process still goes on. In 1960 the reform of the Roman Breviary and Missal entailed a similar reform in the liturgical books of dioceses and religious Orders possessing a rite of their own.

variants are all really Roman "at bottom" (as Edmund Bishop remarked) and that as the Roman rite evolves in the course of the centuries to meet the various needs of different periods and circumstances so must its established variants evolve also.

One other point requires mention at this stage. Much has frequently been made in the past of what has been termed the "rigid uniformity" of Rome in the matter of worship. The information contained in this short book may help perhaps to dispel this mistaken notion. Throughout the territory where the Roman rite is used it will be seen that while the Roman Missal is by far the most extensively used, variations are to be encountered in the churches of certain dioceses and religious Orders. Even in Italy, within a short distance of Rome itself, may be found a rite—the Ambrosian—which exhibits more differences from the usual Roman liturgy than any other Latin rite in considerable use at the present day. Even Latin is not used exclusively, for not so very far from Rome, in Jugoslavia, may be found churches where the Roman Missal is used in a "Church Slavonic" translation (this is referred to shortly here in Appendix III).

After all, it is unity, not uniformity, that is important, and to confuse the two is to introduce an alien notion into the discussion of these matters. It is likely that in the future the Roman rite will evolve in the direction of allowing greater rather than lesser local variations. As races develop and achieve maturity, as the Church's message penetrates among peoples with ancient cultures and traditions, it may be found necessary to adopt measures that were unthought of not so very long ago. Within the last few years vernacular Hebrew has been allowed to five priests in Israel for the first part of Mass and for the Divine Office and permission has been granted to China for the use of a Chinese Missal. These are probably only preliminary steps which may well lead to local adaptations of the Roman rite in these countries on a scale hitherto unimagined.

We seem to have emerged now from the period of "fossiliza-tion" of the Roman rite, a time when not only were the principles of liturgical development obscured in the minds of many but the whole idea of what the liturgy really is and what is its function was wholly misunderstood. At such a time as this, therefore, liturgical studies have come to occupy again a place of importance not allowed to them for some centuries; nowadays they are not, as they were for too long, equated with a study of rubrics. The evolution of the Roman rite continues and will continue because it is the expression of the worship of a living body, the Church.

CHAPTER II

THE AMBROSIAN AND MOZARABIC RITES

The earliest liturgy in the West was Greek and it was only towards the close of the second century that Latin came to be used in worship in North Africa. In Rome the change to Latin occurred between the third and sixth century—it was a gradual process beginning, possibly, with the translation of earlier Greek texts followed by compositions directly in Latin as needs and opportunities required. The first period of the history of the Mass in Latin is obscure and we have little or no evidence that takes us back beyond, at the earliest, the end of the fifth century. Nevertheless, it is possible to discern two liturgical families in the West, the Roman (Romano-African) and the Gallican. Fr J. A. Jungmann, S.J., writes:

In the West there were two large areas, each of which possessed its own liturgical order: Rome and North Africa on the one hand, and the rest of Europe on the other. We can, therefore, call one the Romano-African liturgy, and group all the remaining liturgies under the title of liturgies of the Gallic type or the Gallic liturgies, because Gaul seems somehow to have taken a leading part. ... The Gallic liturgies covered the entire territory from the Iberian peninsula, over Gaul, up to the Danube countries. The British Isles and Upper Italy also belonged to this domain; for the latter was called Gallia Cisalpina. Within this large territory there was not one liturgy but rather one common liturgical system. Everywhere, more or less the same feasts were celebrated and the same liturgical order was basic for the celebration of Mass. But the prayer texts varied from country to country. The one point all had in common was the principle of no fixed canon in regard to the priest's prayers; no prayers were to recur constantly, Mass after Mass, without change (as is the case with our Roman liturgy) with the exception, of course, of the words of consecration, the *Pater noster* and a few other formulas. Each feast, each votive Mass, had its own Mass formulary from the beginning to the end; and these Mass formularies were not one single solemn prayer, a rounded out anaphora, as in the liturgy of the Orient; each Mass formulary was divided into a lengthy series of individual prayers. For example, after the Gospel came the reading of the names of the *offerentes,* followed by a prayer *Post nomina;* then came the kiss of peace and a prayer *Post pacem.* Then came the preface, which was here called *immolatio* or *contestatio;* then the *Sanctus,* followed by a prayer *Post Sanctus;* then the words of consecration beginning with *Pridie quam pateretur* and after that a prayer *Post pridie* (elsewhere called *Post secreta*). (*The Early Liturgy,* pp. 227–8.)

It is usual to distinguish four different liturgies of Gallican type—the Milanese or Ambrosian, Old Spanish or Mozarabic, the Gallican proper (that is, the liturgy of the Germano-Frankish empire) and the Celtic. These were certainly not the only independent forms: "on borderlines, for example in the Danubian countries, there may have been still different shapes and forms . . . " (Jungmann, *op. cit.,* p. 229).

THE AMBROSIAN RITE

Of these four Gallican types of liturgy the only one that now survives as a vigorous growth is the Ambrosian rite of Milan. After some fifteen centuries of existence cheek by jowl with the Roman rite, which for long has been predominant throughout the West, it was inevitable that certain Roman elements should have crept into the Ambrosian rite; nevertheless, it still exhibits certain Gallican features, as we shall see below in the description of the Mass rite.

Origins and history

There has been much discussion on the origin not only of the Ambrosian rite but of all the liturgies of Gallican type; indeed it has been maintained that this liturgical family came in the first place from Milan. In examining the origins of this liturgy, therefore, we shall be dealing to some extent with those of the Mozarabic and other Gallican rites.

An opinion that enjoyed popularity for some time, especially because it lent itself to an anti-Roman interpretation of liturgical history in the West, was that the Gallican liturgy could be traced back to apostolic origins in Ephesus whence it had spread to the West through the influence of the see of Lyons which first adopted it. The difficulty encountered by this theory (among whose supporters may be mentioned Lebrun, J. M. Neale and William Palmer) is that the archetype of this liturgy does not appear to have been in use until the late fourth century and at that time the influence of Lyons was not predominant; indeed in the fifth century Lyons itself was a centre of "Romanization" liturgically.

In his well-known *Christian Worship, Its Origin and Evolution*[1] Mgr Duchesne put forward the hypothesis that Milan was the centre from which the Gallican rite originally came to the West from an eastern source. He adduces in favour of this the fact that in the fourth century Milan was the residence of the emperors and at that period its influence extended as far afield as Spain. Then, too, several of the bishops of Milan came from the East and this, he held, could explain the oriental influence to be discerned in these Gallican type

[1] English translation, 5th edn, pp. 90–5. See Select Bibliography.

liturgies. This hypothesis, though attractive in many ways, still leaves unanswered many difficulties.

One of these is the fact that great changes must have occurred at Milan even as early as St Ambrose, for he describes a canon of the Mass that is fundamentally Roman. It seems that the whole question has been bedevilled at the outset by the fact of identifying the Ambrosian rite with the Gallican. There is no doubt of course that it exhibits "Gallican" characteristics, but it is very possible that these were acquired during the exile of the Church of Milan at Genoa, and that fundamentally the Ambrosian rite is Roman, representing a form of that rite before the changes that took place in the fifth–sixth centuries. In other words, the Ambrosian rite has preserved intact one of the oldest forms of Western liturgy and it is not difficult to see why this should be. It appears that Latin was used as a liturgical language not only in Africa but also in Milan and that this city enjoyed a certain prestige on account of its being for a time the capital of the Empire at the precise moment when St Ambrose was its bishop; his influential position was due not only to his eminence as a leading churchman but also to his fame as a preacher and teacher and his capabilities as a translator who could clothe the prayer of the Church in felicitous language. Of course, no one would maintain that St Ambrose was the actual founder of the rite that bears his name; yet much of its prestige is connected with his great reputation, and some of its text may well have been from his pen.

The present position reached by liturgical research on the question of origins can best be summarized by saying that though the Gallican liturgy has often been ascribed to Milanese origins and the Ambrosian rite regarded as a fourth-century importation from the East, recent scholarship tends to regard the different surviving Western liturgies as later variations on an earlier, more or less uniform rite of the first centuries whose primitive characteristics were best preserved in the Gallican usages.

The reform that took place in Rome was one of abbreviation in the direction of simplicity and sobriety; in its new form the Roman rite eventually spread all over Italy, passed the Alps and finally was made the basis of liturgical unity in the Empire under Charlemagne. In his efforts at liturgical uniformity he was unable, however, to woo the Milanese away from their liturgy. In the eleventh century, at the time of the transplantation of the Romano-Frankish (or Rhenish) liturgy in Rome, little change was made at Milan, though it is true that in the course of centuries certain later Roman developments have not been without their effect on the Ambrosian rite.

In general, the development of the Ambrosian rite shows a clearly-marked stability; this is noteworthy during the Middle Ages which, particularly in the later centuries, were a period of liturgical anarchy. Milan, of course, did not entirely escape the trends of the times and certain liturgical deformations took place in the Ambrosian rite as elsewhere, especially in such matters as the overloading of the calendar with feasts of saints. With the coming of St Charles Borromeo (archbishop, 1560–84), at the very period when the Roman liturgy underwent a major reform, changes were to be expected at Milan also, but St Charles proved a staunch defender of the Ambrosian rite, pointing out that instead of the two centuries required by the Bull *Quod a nobis* it could show upwards of one thousand years of continued existence. Of course, as with all rites at this and other periods of general liturgical reform, the changes in the Roman rite had some effect at Milan, but what was done there in the sixteenth century was no more than was inevitable in a living rite; the Sunday Office was given greater prominence and the calendar was lightened in order to leave nearly two hundred days free for the ferial Office. A simplified classification of feasts was introduced (three classes: *solemnes, simplices* and *privilegiati*) and in accordance with primitive practice their celebration was forbidden in Lent.

The typical edition of the Missal appeared in 1902. It was the work of Antonio Ceriani and Achille Ratti (later Pius XI) who had carried out a careful scrutiny of the ninth- and tenth-century manuscripts in order to reproduce as faithfully as possible the authentic Ambrosian liturgy.

The order of Mass

Mass begins at Milan, as at Rome, with the singing of an entrance chant, the accompaniment of the procession of clergy entering the sanctuary. At Milan this chant is called *Ingressa* and, from both name and function, would seem to correspond with the introit of the Roman Missal; but it differs in that the introit was originally a chant with a complete psalm concluded with the doxology and the repetition of the antiphon. The *Ingressa* is a chant without psalm, doxology or repetition.

The prayers at the foot of the altar are substantially the same as those in the Roman Missal; in the Ambrosian Missal, as in the Roman, they are an addition that was made in the Middle Ages. The name of St Ambrose is added to the saints in the *Confiteor*, but Ps. 42 is not said. The celebrant goes up to the altar and incenses it. On Sundays and feast dàys the *Gloria in excelsis* follows and to this is added a threefold *Kyrie eleison* (*Christe eleison* is not said at Milan). Then, as in the Roman rite, come the collect and the lessons. The collect, known as the prayer over the people (*oratio super populum*) is of the same form as the Roman collects and in many cases is textually identical. There are three lessons at Mass in the Ambrosian rite and this seems to have been the practice at Rome in early times.[2] The first lesson is taken

[2] Cf. in the Roman rite the Wednesdays and Fridays in Ember weeks or, in the Dominican and Carthusian liturgies and others of medieval origin, the prophetical lesson on Christmas Eve and Christmas day. See Amiot, *op. cit.*, p. 50.

from the Old Testament or sometimes from the *acta* of the martyrs, the second corresponds to the Epistle in the Roman rite and the third is the Gospel. Between the first and second lessons occurs the chant known as *psalmellus* (that is, little psalm). Alleluia and verse come between Epistle and Gospel. The Roman gradual and Alleluia would seem to be the combination of two chants that were originally separate. The Gospel is sung by the deacon with ceremonial similar to that appointed in the Roman rite, but from the same ambo as the Epistle.

After the Gospel and sermon, if there is one, the celebrant once more greets the congregation with *Dominus vobiscum* and, unlike the Roman rite, there immediately follows a collect *super sindonem* (over the corporal). The *Dominus vobiscum* at the offertory in the Roman rite standing by itself has been seen by many as the only relic of the former "prayer of the faithful" [3] but it is not at all certain and other liturgists, such as Edmund Bishop, regard the *oratio super sindonem* as an element that has disappeared from the Roman rite but has been retained by the Ambrosian. This prayer is part of the proper of the Mass in the Ambrosian Missal and is of the usual collect form.

At this point at the cathedral of Milan occurs a ceremony that is known as the most distinctive custom of the Ambrosian rite. Ten old men (*vecchioni*) dressed in a traditional and, to modern eyes, somewhat strange costume (it consists of a long cloak with a hood), come forward; the two leaders bear three hosts in the right hand and a silver cruet in the left; they ask the celebrant's blessing and then present their offering. At the entrance to the lower choir the same ceremony is performed by ten old women. These *vecchioni* belong to the Scuola of St Ambrose and are supported by the chapter of the cathedral. Meanwhile the offertory chant is sung.

At the altar the celebrant receives the paten from the deacon

[3] This view is put forward by Amiot, *op. cit.*, p. 62.

and offers the host, saying the prayer *Suscipe, clementissime Pater, hunc panem sanctum*: "Accept, most merciful Father, this sacred bread that it may become the body of your only-begotten Son, in the name of the Father and of the Son and of the Holy Ghost." Putting wine and water into the chalice he says: *De latere Domini nostri* . . . : "From the side of our Lord Jesus Christ came forth blood and water for the remission of sins, in the name of the Father and of the Son and of the Holy Ghost." [4] After a short prayer of offering (analogous with the offering of the host) and a further prayer (*Omnipotens sempiterne Deus*) said bowing low, there follow two prayers (*Suscipe sancta Trinitas . . . Et suscipe sancta Trinitas*) which strongly resemble those of the Roman rite. The incensing of the altar follows Roman practice with similar formulas save for that used in returning the thurible to the deacon. The latter then incenses the rear of the altar and kisses it; this incensing is continued by the thurifer during the *Credo* which now follows. The *Oratio super oblata* (the prayer over the offerings) corresponds with the secret in the Roman rite. The offertory prayers just described are all of medieval origin and are taken, like those at this point in the Roman rite, from the private devotions formerly recommended for the use of the laity present at Mass.

At the end of the *Oratio super oblata* the celebrant sings *Per omnia saecula saeculorum* and the usual versicles introducing the preface, which varies far more frequently than in the Roman rite. The canon, save for the two lists of saints at the *Communicantes* and *Nobis quoque peccatoribus*, is the Roman canon with certain very slight variants. At the *Communicantes*, after the Apostles the celebrant commemorates instead of Linus, Cletus, etc., Hippolytus and Vincent, Apollinaris, Vitalis, Nazarus and Celsus, Protase and Gervase, Victor, Nabor, Felix, Calimerus. For the most part these are local saints. Certain of the verbal differences in the canon require

[4] Cf. Lyons and Carthusian rites.

to be noticed. In the *Hanc igitur* instead of *placatus accipias* there is *placatus suscipias;* in the *Quam oblationem: quam pietati tuae offerimus, tu, Deus, in omnibus quaesumus....* Immediately after this prayer the celebrant washes his hands in silence; this ceremony is not found before the thirteenth century. At the consecration the following variations occur: in *Qui pridie pateretur* we find *pro nostra omniumque salute* (cf. the Roman rite on Maundy Thursday); the consecration of the chalice is followed by *Mandans quoque et dicens ad eos....*: "Commanding them and telling them: as often as you do these things you shall do them in memory of me. You shall preach my death, you shall announce my resurrection, you shall hope in my coming until I come to you again from heaven" (Cf. 1 Cor. 2. 26).

During the *Unde et memores* the celebrant extends his arms in the form of a cross; this is a common medieval practice still to be found nowadays in the Lyons and the monastic rites. The three prayers following the elevation, save for certain very slight variations of a word here and there, are the same as in the Roman rite.[5]

The memento of the dead is the same as in the Roman rite but the *Nobis quoque peccatoribus* shows the following differences: the beginning of the prayer reads *Nobis quoque minimis, et peccatoribus, famulis tuis;* the saints mentioned are not entirely the same for we find John (the Evangelist), John (the Baptist), Andrew (instead of Matthias), Barnabas, Peter, Marcellinus, Agnes, Cecily, Felicity, Perpetua, Anastasia, Agatha, Euphemia, Lucy, Justina, Sabina, Thecla, Pelagia and Catherine.

The Lord's Prayer (sung as in the Roman rite) is followed by the *Libera* (slight verbal differences and the addition of the name of St Ambrose) which is also sung. The fraction precedes the Lord's Prayer and occurs therefore at the conclusion of

---

[5] For example: *gloriosissimae ascensionis* in the *Unde et memores; vultu tuo* in the *Supra quae; tremendae majestatis* in the *Supplices.*

the canon. As he divides the host the celebrant says: *Corpus tuum frangitur . . .* ("Your body is broken, O Christ, your chalice is blessed") and *Sanguis tuus . . .* ("May your blood ever avail us for life and the salvation of our souls"). There is then sung an anthem (one of the variable chants of the Mass) known as the *Confractorium* (that is, the chant at the fraction). The formula at the commixture is *Commixtio consecrati corporis et sanguinis . . .* ("May the commixture of the consecrated body and blood of our Lord Jesus Christ avail us for everlasting life and joy").

After the *Libera* the celebrant sings *Pax et communicatio Domini nostri Jesus Christi sit semper vobiscum*; following the response the deacon sings *Offerte vobis pacem* and then, after the prayer *Domine Jesu Christe* (as in the Roman rite) the Pax is given. There is no *Agnus Dei* save in Masses for the Dead. The prayers before the Communion are similar to those in the Lyons and Dominican rites. At the Communion of the congregation the celebrant says merely to each communicant *Corpus Christi* as he gives him the host; the communicant answers *Amen*.[6] During the distribution of Communion the choir sings the *Transitorium* which corresponds to the communion anthem of the Roman rite. The postcommunion (*Oratio post communionem* in the Ambrosian rite) is followed by *Dominus vobiscum*, threefold *Kyrie eleison, Benedicat et exaudiat nos Deus* ("May God bless us and hear us") and the monition from the deacon, *Procedamus in pace* ("Let us go forth in peace") with the answer *In nomine Christi, Amen* ("In the name of Christ, Amen"); then *Benedicamus Domino* (never *Ite, missa est*), *Placeat* (slightly different from the Roman), the blessing and last Gospel.

[6] Cf. St Ambrose: "When you come forward the priest says to you 'The Body of Christ' and you answer 'Amen', that is, 'It is true'." (*De Sacramentis*, IV, 25: Migne, *Patrologia Latina*, 16, 417). Migne, *Patrologia Latina* is quoted hereafter as Migne, *P.L.* followed by volume and column number.

The liturgical year 1171955

The Ambrosian Missal provides a very large selection not only of chants for the choir (*Ingressa, Psalmellus, Confractorium, Transitorium*, etc.) but of proper prefaces, *Communicantes*, etc., for the celebrant. In this respect it is far richer than the Roman Missal and betrays thereby something of its origins.

The liturgical year begins with Advent, the first Sunday of which is that nearest to the feast of St Martin (November 11th); there are consequently six Sundays in Advent, the last of which is a commemoration of the Annunciation. Lent begins on the first Sunday, and there is no Ash Wednesday (or blessing of ashes) and the fast begins on the first Monday. Saturdays in Lent are non-fasting days and the Fridays are aliturgical days—days, that is, on which Mass is not celebrated, though in recent times permission has been granted for the celebration of the feasts of St Joseph (March 19th) and the Annunciation (March 25th) should one or other of them occur on a Friday. The Ambrosian calendar in fact contains few feasts during the season in which Lent occurs.

The Sundays in Lent are known by the subjects of their Gospels. After the first (*in capite Quadragesimae*), there occurs *De Samaritana, De Abraham, De Caeco* and *De Lazaro*.[7] On these after the *Ingressa* there is a litany with a collect. Two forms are given in the Missal and these are recited on alternate Sundays. Here there is a great resemblance with the Eastern rites but there is resemblance also with the primitive practice in the Roman rite and an allusion may be found to it in Tertullian's description of a prayer for all conditions.[8]

The celebration of Holy Week differs very largely from Roman practice. On Maundy Thursday, for example, there is

[7] *De Lazaro* is the fifth Sunday; Passiontide begins only on the sixth, Palm Sunday.
[8] *De oratione*, 29. See also Amiot, *op. cit.*, pp. 37–8.

a service of readings and prayers after Terce; the Mass in commemoration of the institution of the Lord's Supper is joined to solemn Vespers. The Passion is not read at Mass during Holy Week except for St Matthew which is appointed to be read half on Maundy Thursday and half on Good Friday. The others have their place in the Breviary Office. There is no provision for Communion on Good Friday in the *editio typica* of the Missal (1902) as the Office there appointed contains no "Mass of the Presanctified" as did the Roman Missal up to recent times, but once again, there is a service of lessons and prayers; on Good Friday this concludes with the veneration of the cross.

The Sundays after Pentecost are divided into four series: fifteen "after Pentecost", five after the Beheading of St John the Baptist, three Sundays of October, the last of which is the Dedication of the Great Church and three Sundays after the Dedication.[9]

In the course of a few pages it has been impossible to give more than a summary picture of the ancient rite of Milan. Enough has been said however to show that despite a certain amount of "Romanization" in the last six or seven hundred years, the Ambrosian liturgy preserves its essential and very ancient features and offers an example of what the Roman liturgy may have been before the time of St Gregory the Great.

THE MOZARABIC RITE

At the present time the Mozarabic rite is performed, somewhat perfunctorily, in a chapel of the cathedral at Toledo and remains thus as a mere relic of the former liturgy of the Church in Spain. Yet it is worthy of study on many grounds,

[9] If Easter is late and there is not room for fifteen Sundays after Pentecost those for which there is no room before the Beheading of St John the Baptist (August 29th) are omitted that year.

not least because it is a "homogeneous liturgy, built up according to clearly stated principles".[10]

Origins and history

The origins of the Mozarabic liturgy remain obscure. It is a liturgy of Gallican type in the sense that it is similar to the forms prevalent in Gaul before the imposition of the Roman rite by Charlemagne. Because when they first settled in Spain the Visigoths were already Christians, though Arians, it has been suggested that their liturgy was of eastern origin. It seems more likely, however, that Roman and African elements already in use in Spain were taken by the seventh-century bishops and re-modelled by them with a generous admixture of usages from neighbouring Gaul and with the addition of prayers and prefaces which they composed themselves. The late W. C. Bishop has summed up the whole question of the origin of all these rites (Ambrosian, Gallican, Mozarabic) admirably:

> In treating the Mozarabic Mass it is impossible to exclude consideration of the Gallican Mass, for this was but a variant of the same rite; and the same may be said of the (original) Celtic Mass. Indeed this rite (so far as our information goes) seems to have been originally the rite of the whole Latin Church, with the exception of the city of Rome and its immediate environs. Even in Africa the lectionary which underlies St Augustine's sermons is clearly of a Gallican and not of a Roman type: the same may be said of the liturgical fragments preserved in quotation; and the only point in which the African liturgy clearly agreed with the Roman as against the Gallican was the position of the *Pax* after the consecration. . . .
>
> Mgr Duchesne, in *Origines du culte chrétien,* has attempted to solve the problem as to whence the Gallican liturgy spread into Gaul and Spain, but we venture to think that he has altogether mistaken the nature of the problem. The "Gallican" rite was the original rite of the West, and its introduction needs

[10] I.-H. Dalmais, O.P.: *Introduction to the Liturgy,* p. 176.

no accounting for. If, as he supposes, it was introduced into the West only at the end of the fourth century, the question immediately arises, "What rite did the Christians use before that date?"—a question without answer, for it is absurd to suppose that there was any earlier rite in these parts.[11]

The great names connected with the Mozarabic rite and its development in the sixth to eighth centuries are Eugenius, Ildephonsus and Julian; they composed Masses and hymns and the last-named revised the Sacramentary, adding to it considerably.

All accounts of this rite deal with the question of its orthodoxy. The question arises because of the prevalence of the Adoptionist heresy in Spain where its chief representatives were Elipandus, archbishop of Toledo, and Felix, bishop of Urgel. In defence of their views they urged that the liturgy, by employing the terms *adoptio* and *adoptivus*, supported their teaching that Christ was the Son of God only by adoption and grace. It is now admitted that the Mozarabic liturgy is perfectly orthodox and indeed the fact of its survival today with the continued use of the expressions quoted by the heretical bishops shows that these terms possess an orthodox meaning. Dom Guéranger's suggestion that the rite underwent a purification in the eighth century in order to achieve orthodoxy has no evidence to support it and the fact that the equivocal expressions still remain is an insuperable obstacle in the way of any such theory. That prayers from a liturgy have been quoted in support of a heresy is by no means evidence of the presence of heresy in it any more than the wresting of biblical texts from their context proves that the Bible contains erroneous doctrine.

The rite was suppressed throughout Spain in the eleventh century, though at differing dates in the various kingdoms then

[11] W. C. Bishop: *The Mozarabic and Ambrosian Rites* (London and Milwaukee, 1924), p. 20. This statement should be compared with what is said above, pp. 25 following.

in existence. The centralizing tendencies of the Gregorian reform (combined with the spreading to Spain of the Cluniac monks who propagated the Roman rite) encouraged the abolition of the Mozarabic rite.

Despite the attachment of the Toledans to their liturgy (after the death of Gregory VII six parishes of Toledo were allowed to retain the Mozarabic rite) in the course of the later Middle Ages the liturgical manuscripts became increasingly illegible and, when no longer serviceable, were not replaced so that many Roman formulas and customs were introduced and, in addition, the number of those belonging to the rite (the "Mozarabs") diminished considerably. By the end of the fifteenth century the Mozarabic rite had practically disappeared and was celebrated only on the more important festivals. That it has survived until the present time (though it can hardly be said to be flourishing) is due to Cardinal Francisco Ximenes de Cisneros who became archbishop of Toledo in 1495. He it was who gave orders for the printing of the liturgical books; the Missal appeared in 1500. This revival was not entirely successful and in spite of Cardinal de Cisneros's foundations the number of parishioners of the rite continued to diminish. Other causes, too, were at work. The political troubles of the nineteenth century and finally the Civil War of 1936–9 practically extinguished the traditional Spanish rite. It was restored again in 1940 when provision was made for six chaplains to perform the liturgy daily in the chapel of Corpus Christi at the cathedral of Toledo. Daily Office and Mass in the Mozarabic rite are thus said nowadays in one church but all the evidence seems to show that there is little enthusiasm for it and that it is hardly more than a ritual gesture, a lifeless restoration of merely archeological interest.

The term Mozarabic is in reality a misnomer for the rite was in existence in Spain before the Arab conquest in 712. Mozarabic (from *musta'rab*, "mixed with the Arabs") applies, properly speaking, only to those of the Spanish population who submitted to the Arab domination and the rite was in use among the free Spaniards of the North. But the name is now well established and to call the rite the Visigothic rite, Spanish rite or rite of Toledo would be merely pedantic and not entirely correct.

The order of Mass

At the foot of the altar the celebrant intones an antiphon: "For the glory of your name, O Christ, Son of the living God, and through the intercession of Blessed Mary and all your saints, be pleased to help and pity your unworthy servants and dwell in their midst, you who are God, living and reigning, etc." To this the choir replies, *Deo gratias*. Then, after Psalm 42, *Confiteor*, versicles and prayer *Aufer a nobis*, more or less as in the Roman rite, he goes up to the altar, kisses it, spreads the corporal, places upon it host and chalice (in which wine and water have already been prepared) and censes the oblations. It will be seen at once that some of these elements are ancient and that others of them are of more recent introduction from the Roman rite. Formerly the preparation of the chalice took place at the offertory.

The Mass begins properly speaking with the entrance chant (called in the Mozarabic rite *Officium*) which resembles the Roman introit very closely. The ancient *Liber Ordinum* directs the celebrant to say before the *Officium* a prayer that Christ present in the Eucharist as "a burning coal" may cleanse his lips as he did those of Isaias, but this prayer has now been displaced to a position after the Gospel. The *Gloria in excelsis*, collect and lessons follow. There are three of these latter, prophecy, Epistle and Gospel with, before each, an admonition to the people by the deacon to keep silence. The ceremonies at the Gospel are very much like those of the Roman rite from which they are an early borrowing. Formerly in the Mozarabic rite it was the celebrant who sang the Gospel as is the practice in the Byzantine rite.

After the Gospel is sung the *lauda* or *laudes,* a chant which is thought to have been formerly the accompaniment of the offertory procession like the offertory anthem in the Roman rite. During it the celebrant offers host and chalice with four short prayers that are importations from the Roman rite though they differ from those actually prescribed in the Missal of St Pius V. The altar is then incensed and the priest says or sings *Orate fratres; adjuvate me, fratres, in orationibus vestris et orate pro me ad Deum* ("Pray, brethren; assist me, brethren with your prayers and pray for me to God").

At this point occurs a further antiphon or responsory called *sacrificium.* Originally it was sung while the gifts, brought to the altar in procession during the singing of the *lauda,* were placed upon the altar. (There are one or two examples in the Roman rite of offertory anthems in responsorial form: cf. for example that in the Mass for the Dead.) The *Lavabo* follows. Mass now continues with the seven great prayers which form part of the proper of the Mass, that is they vary every day. Between them are said certain fixed parts of the order of Mass so that it is necessary for the celebrant to have open before him two books, a *Missale omnium offerentium* [12] for the fixed parts and a complete Missal for the variables. Before we see how these great prayers are fitted into the Mass it will be well to have a list of them so that when they occur they can be distinguished from the invariable parts of the Mass. They are *Missa, Alia, Post nomina, Ad pacem, Illatio, Post pridie* and *Ad orationem dominicam.* These seven prayers certainly go back to before the time of St Isidore (†636) who mentions them as already traditional in his day.

The *Missa* is usually fairly long and is sometimes in the form of an exhortation to the people. Between the *Missa* and the next prayer occurs a short litany. It has two clauses praying for the Church and all conditions of men and is introduced by the choir singing, "*Agios, agios, agios,* Lord God, eternal

[12] There is no very adequate explanation for this name.

King, to you be thanks and praise." [13] The *Alia* (sc. *oratio*) follows; it leads up to the diptychs the first of which commemorates the Apostles and martyrs. The second diptych is announced as *Item pro spiritibus pausantium* ("Also for the souls of the waiting ones"). In this are included the names of confessors together with those of Toledan bishops, not all of whom have been canonized. There follows the third variable prayer, the *Post nomina*, which is said for those present or for the faithful departed.

At this point, as in the Eastern liturgies, follows the kiss of peace, preceded by the fourth variable prayer, *Ad pacem*. Then comes the dialogue leading up to the eucharistic prayer properly so called. It is a little more elaborate than the dialogue before the preface in the Roman rite and is followed by the *Illatio*, which corresponds to the Roman preface though it is much longer than any proper preface in the Roman Missal. This is the fifth of the variable prayers so that it is true to say that every Mass in the Mozarabic rite has its own preface. The following is an example of the *Illatio* (from the second Sunday after the octave of the Epiphany):

> It is meet and right, our blessed and bounden duty, at all times to render thanks to you, God Almighty; in your name both celebrating the mysteries of our solemnities and offering to you this sacrifice (simple to offer, rich to partake) which the highest praises cannot worthily proclaim. Here is neither the bleating of sheep nor the bellowing of cattle nor the death cry of fluttering fowl to grieve the ear. Here the eye is not shocked with blood nor the appetite with surfeit; yet so wonderful and astounding is the victim that though without blood it is eaten alive. For though the true body is eaten and the blood most manifestly drunk yet nevertheless without aught distasteful is the salvation of our souls ministered in the spiritual food and cup. For blessed is your Son, our Lord Jesus Christ, who coming in your name commanded that these sacrifices should

---

[13] Ἅγιος, ἅγιος, ἅγιος, *Domine Deus, rex aeterne, tibi laudes et gratias*. This bilingual form is probably an importation into the rite.

be presented before you. Mindful of his precepts we both keep his commandments and commemorate his mighty deeds, whom with you and the Holy Spirit the hosts of earth and heaven duly unite to praise, with cherubim and seraphim ever more praising you and saying. . . .[14]

The *Illatio* leads up to the *Sanctus* and *Benedictus* [15]; these are followed by a variable prayer, the *Post Sanctus,* which serves as a transition between the *Sanctus* and the consecration. Formerly it was simple in form and led straight to the words of institution: "Truly holy, truly blessed is our Lord Jesus Christ, who on the day before he suffered . . . ." But in the Mozarabic Missal at a quite early date the *Post Sanctus* was elaborated and an interpolation was made after it of a prayer, *Adesto, Jesu bone,* which breaks the sequence. (The *Adesto* was almost certainly at first a private prayer of the celebrant's.) Directly after this short prayer the words of institution follow, but they are introduced by the formula *Dominus noster Jesus Christus in qua nocte tradebatur* as in the East, instead of the formula, everywhere prevalent in the West, *Qui pridie.* That in the Mozarabic rite originally the form *Qui pridie* was used can be seen from the fact that immediately after the elevation of the chalice the sixth variable prayer is called *Post pridie.* At what date the change was made is unknown. The *Post pridie* is seen by Dom Cabrol as corresponding to the epiclesis in the Eastern liturgies, at least in some instances, though certain of the formulas of this prayer on some days of the year contain no allusion to anything that could be seen as an epiclesis. The *Post pridie* is followed by a short prayer which corresponds to the Roman *Per quem haec omnia* at the end of the canon and leads up to the "little elevation"

[14] This is the translation, slightly amended, by W. C. Bishop, *op. cit.,* pp. 37–8.

[15] These vary slightly from the Roman text: *Sanctus, sanctus sanctus Dominus Deus Sabaoth: pleni sunt caeli et terra gloria majestatis tuae: Hosanna Filio David, Hosanna in excelsis. Benedictus qui venit in nomine Domini. Hosanna in excelsis.*

of the host as the celebrant says: "The faith which we believe in our hearts let us confess with our mouths."

This is the introduction to the creed which is said at this point; as the priest says it in a low voice while the choir sings it he holds the host over the chalice. There are a certain number of variations from the form now usual in the West.[16] If there is no creed (it is omitted for example in Lent) an anthem is sung at this point (*antiphona ad confractorium*) while the priest performs the fraction, otherwise he does so during the creed.

In the Mozarabic rite the fraction is exceedingly complicated. The host is divided into nine particles. These are arranged on the paten in the form of a cross and to each particle a name of a mystery in our Lord's life is given. The following is the arrangement with the names:

	CORPORATIO	
MORS	NATIVITAS	RESURRECTIO
	CIRCUMCISIO	
	APPARITIO	GLORIA
	PASSIO	REGNUM

As may be imagined all sorts of mystical and symbolical interpretations of this practice have been essayed in the past and also a certain number of abuses in connection with it have arisen. When the fraction is finished the priest with hands joined makes a memento of the living, saying aloud *Memento pro vivis*. There is no formula for this and indeed it is a duplication of the prayers at an earlier stage of the Mass.

The seventh and last of the great variable prayers is that called *Ad orationem Dominicam* because it is said before the Lord's Prayer to which it forms the introduction. That for the

---

[16] It is said in the plural number (*Credimus*); note especially the use of the formula of the Council of Nicaea: *Deum ex Deo, Lumen ex lumine, Deum verum ex Deo vero. Natum, non factum omousion Patri, hoc est, ejusdem cum Patre substantiae.* "Omousion" is of course the Greek ὁμούσιον.

second Sunday after the octave of the Epiphany shows its hortatory character: "Beloved brethren, mindful of the Lord's commandments, let us repeat the words of the Lord's Prayer, suppliantly imploring his majesty that he would mercifully forget our offences and sanctify our hearts and bodies with the gift of his grace; so that purged from every spot of sin, with free voices we may cry from earth (Our Father ...)."

The Lord's Prayer is sung by the celebrant alone but after each petition the congregation answers Amen. After the embolism, as in the Roman rite a development of the theme of the last petition of the Lord's Prayer, has been sung by the celebrant the commixture follows. The priest takes the particle *Regnum* and holding it over the chalice says, "Holy things to the holy, and may the union (*conjunctio*) of the body of our Lord Jesus Christ avail for pardon to us who eat and drink, and for peace to the faithful departed."

Before the communion there is a blessing preceded by a diaconal monition, "Bow your heads for blessing". Then, after the blessing (there are usually five clauses) the choir sings an anthem called *Ad accedentes,* that is, with reference to those who are about to communicate. Formerly at this point the deacon had said *Locis vestris accedite* ("Come forward to your places") but this is now omitted for a reason that will appear clearly in the next paragraph. Meanwhile with suitable prayers (as in the Roman rite, a late introduction) the priest communicates, receiving the particle *Gloria* and then the chalice; finally he consumes the remaining particles on the paten.

Holy Communion is no longer given in the Mozarabic rite which, as one authority says "has degenerated into a mere archaeological survival with little or not *raison d'être.*" It can only be supposed that there is now no congregation attached to the Mozarabic rite for it hardly seems credible that they should thus be virtually excommunicated. After the ablutions the Mass concludes with a prayer called *Completuria,* that is the postcommunion, and the dismissal by the deacon, usually in this form: *Missa acta est in nomine Domini Jesu Christi, perficiamus in pace* ("Mass is ended in the name of our Lord Jesus Christ. Let us depart in peace").

This account of the rite of the Mozarabic Mass has been given in some detail because, despite the hybrid nature of some of its features, in it can be clearly discerned the pattern of the ancient Gallican liturgy which prevailed in Christian Europe north of the Alps before the introduction of the Roman rite under Charlemagne. For that reason it is important for it preserves a form of worship that before Charlemagne's reforms was widespread in the West.

CHAPTER III

THE RITES OF LYONS
AND BRAGA

In the previous chapter we considered two autonomous liturgies, those of Milan and Toledo. We come now to the two
remaining diocesan liturgies which are not autonomous rites
at all but merely variants of the Roman rite, representing its
state at one stage of its development. Speaking of these rites
(together with those of the Carmelites and Dominicans) Dom
Cabrol writes:

> Not only are they all derived from the Roman liturgy, but
> some of them are purely and simply that liturgy just as it
> existed from the eleventh–thirteenth centuries before it under-
> went certain reforms or suffered the changes imposed upon it
> subsequently. The Orders and Churches in question did not
> accept these changes, so that the student today finds himself
> in the presence of a liturgy which is that of Rome between
> the eleventh and thirteenth centuries.[1]

In dealing with these liturgies as they are today it has to be
borne in mind that, as has been pointed out already, they have
subsequently adopted many of the changes that have taken
place in the present rite and have thus moved progressively
nearer to the modern Roman liturgy.

[1] F. Cabrol, *The Mass of the Western Rites* (London, 1934), p. 185.

THE RITE OF LYONS

Origins and history

Dr J. M. Neale, who was an admirable translator of Latin hymns but a somewhat erratic historian of liturgy, wrote of "the generic term Gallican, as opposed to Roman, and signifying that form of liturgy which was apparently derived from Asia Minor (and so from St John) and which received its earliest development in the Church of Lyons". Neale was in good company and could have quoted even Cardinal Bona as a supporter of this theory. It is an attractive one, and proved especially so to the nineteenth-century supporters of the distinctive usages of Lyons when the whole liturgical question was being hotly debated in France and there was considerable danger of the Lyons liturgy disappearing entirely. By linking the origin of their rite with the rites of Ephesus and Smyrna, through St Irenaeus and St Pothinus, sent by St Polycarp, the disciple of St John the Evangelist, the supporters of the Lyons liturgy felt that the position of the antiquity of their rite was impregnable.

Pothinus and Irenaeus, the great names of early Lyonese history, belong in reality to a period when the liturgy was in a rudimentary state and more or less uniform everywhere; since it had hardly developed by that time it was confined almost to essentials. The supporters of this (the so-called Ephesine theory) offer as an alternative theory the importation of Eastern liturgical practices from Asia in the fourth century, but by that time the influence of Lyons was on the wane and there was then no link attaching it to Smyrna or Asia Minor. In fact, of course, there never was an Irenaean liturgy any more than there was a Polycarpian or Johannine liturgy. Theories of this kind are propounded for a variety of reasons and even when discarded have a way of reappearing in respectable places. Thus in 1902 a decree of the Congregation of Rites concerning the new edition of the Lyons Missal stated that "the celebrated Church of Lyons, the most distinguished in France by its antiquity and authority, from the earliest times preserved its own rite which it is said to have received from Irenaeus, its bishop and martyr".[2]

The alternative offered by the partisans of a non-Roman origin of the Lyons rite is that it is derived from the ancient Gallican rite. It cannot be denied that the Mass at Lyons shows certain Gallican traces but then so does the Roman Missal; the presence of certain rites or formulas is no indication of the origin of a whole rite. The special peculiarities of the rite of Lyons seem scarcely at all to recall the features of the Gallican rite as it is to be found in the surviving documents of the seventh and eighth centuries. Before the eighth century the Mass at Lyons may well have belonged to the rite formerly followed in all the Churches of Gaul, but it was certainly not the present rite. Lyons, like the rest of the country, underwent the liturgical revolution effected by Pepin and Charlemagne when they imposed the (Gregorian) Roman rite on the territory under their rule.

The vacancy that occurred in the see of Lyons in about 789 offered a good opportunity for the election of one who would see to the reorganization of the liturgy in the diocese. Charlemagne obtained the election of Leidrade and entrusted him with the task of reforming the liturgy at Lyons according to the model of the palatine chapel at Aachen, that is, in accordance with the Gregorian Roman rite. Leidrade retained a certain number of local usages at Lyons but the whole groundwork of his reform was Roman; it was the Roman liturgy, as it had been shaped by the liturgists at Aachen and Metz, Alcuin among them, that became the liturgy of Lyons. And, of

---

[2] *Nobilis Lugdunensis ecclesia, antiquitate et dignitate in Galliis praestantissima, proprios ritus quos ab Irenaeo praesule suo et martyre accepisse fertur, a priscis temporibus fideliter tenuit.* On the origin of the liturgy of Lyons I am following here Dom Denys Buenner, *L'Ancienne liturgie romaine, le rite lyonnais* (Lyons, 1934), pp. 15–68.

all the Churches of France, Lyons was to show the greatest fidelity to this Roman-Carolingian liturgy.

Leidrade's successor was Agobard (honoured as a saint at Lyons) who ruled the diocese 814–40. He is notorious for his insistence on the principle that nothing but Scripture should be used in the liturgy. He wrote two treatises against Amalarius who had governed the diocese during the bishop's absence and had seized on the opportunity to introduce a new anti-phoner. Agobard mentions in his diatribe against Amalarius [3] "the horrible blasphemies to be found in the antiphoner" and lays down the principle that just as at Mass only scriptural forms are used so too should the same thing be done at the Divine Office.

The chapter of the primatial church (Saint-Jean) was extremely conservative and tenacious of its privileges which it maintained throughout the Middle Ages, adding to them as opportunity offered. The influence of the liturgy of Lyons, also, was great over the neighbouring Churches—Grenoble, Die, Valence, Vienne in particular. St Bruno (see following chapter) adopted the Lyons rite for the hermit-monks founded by him. As an example of the conservatism of the canons of Lyons may be mentioned the hymns of the Breviary. Rome for long admitted no hymns in the Office, nevertheless by the end of the twelfth century they had their place in the Roman anti-phoner. Lyons on the contrary retained the proscription right down to the changes of the eighteenth century; during all the centuries from the ninth onwards no hymns were sung in the cathedral at Lyons save only that for Compline.

But if Lyons was faithful in preserving the Roman-Carolingian liturgical heritage, what has come to be known as the Franco-Roman rite, it must be acknowledged also that other Churches in France at that time were no less faithful: Paris, Rouen, Rheims, Sens and Tours enjoyed for long a similar reputation, and each exerted a more than local influence. Such

[3] Migne, *P.L.* 104, 327.

an influence is to be discerned in the following chapter treating of the rites of the religious Orders. The point of importance here is that we should understand what this Romano-Frankish liturgy was and whence it came. Its origins and shape are to be seen reflected in the liturgy of Lyons.

With the appearance of the reformed Roman Missal (1570) Lyons corrected her own Massbook while carefully preserving her ancient rite. But towards the end of the seventeenth century and during the eighteenth a new current of ideas was abroad. Everywhere in France it had grown fashionable to reform the local liturgical books (how this led to the loss of ancient customs and the imposition of the Roman rite can be seen in Appendix I). The first modifications to the rubrics at Lyons date from 1737 but it was only in 1771 that Mgr de Montazet suppressed the Missal that had been in use since Carolingian times in favour of that drawn up by Mgr de Noailles, the archbishop of Paris. This neo-Gallican composition abolished at one stroke the whole Gregorian foundation of the Missal taking in its place a modern composition with all the faults and disadvantages of the neo-Gallican liturgies.

After the French Revolution Cardinal Fesch (Napoleon's uncle) was archbishop; under his rule and during that of his successor (Mgr de Pins) at the time of the Restoration an attempt was made to restore the old rite; the ceremonies were codified and a beginning was made on the revision of the liturgical books. The intention was to preserve as much as possible of the former ceremonies and to make an attempt to restore the Missal to its former state. Mgr de Pins's successor, Cardinal de Bonald, was antagonistic to the liturgy of Lyons. Unfortunately some of those most strongly in favour of the restoration of the ancient rite were Gallicans; on the pretext of opposing Gallicanism and of achieving an orthodox form of prayer (de Montazet's Missal was said to be tainted with Jansenism), and of returning to the Roman rite, an attempt was made to abolish all the ancient customs of Lyons and to adopt the Roman rite in its actual form. Such a course, needless to say, aroused opposition from the chapter and the parochial clergy and a bitter controversy ensued. Rome also was unsympathetic but in the end Pius IX in 1863 gave his approval to the liturgy of Lyons. What was approved was in reality an adaptation of the Roman Breviary and Missal to the customs of Lyons—it was a substitution, as Dom Buenner says, of the Roman books for those of eighteenth-century Paris. Finally in 1902 Leo XIII approved a Missal in which the Lyons *Ordo Missae,* the local feasts and special customs of the rite were included in their proper places: *Missale Romanum in quo antiqui ritus Lugdunenses servantur, Apostolicae Sedis auctoritate recognitum et probatum,* 1904.

Pontifical Mass

Since the principal differences between the modern Roman rite and that of Lyons are ceremonial rather than ritual, and these differences are to be seen more clearly in the solemn Mass celebrated by the archbishop in his cathedral, it will be clearer to describe the chief features of such a pontifical Mass before examining the *Ordo Missae.* At the outset it may be pointed out that a pontifical Mass celebrated in this way recalls for us what must have been, not at Lyons but all over Europe, the liturgical splendour of the Middle Ages. It is only possible to describe here the principal features of the pontifical Mass, details must be sought in the books mentioned in the select bibliography.

When the archbishop makes his solemn entry after the singing of Terce [4] he is preceded by a long and imposing procession: 1. Seven acolytes with their candles. 2. Two clerks in copes who will later carry the processional cross and the pas-

[4] Terce as an immediate obligatory preparation for a pontifical high Mass is an importation from the modern Roman rite; its use in this way was certainly unknown before the twelfth century. At Lyons, too, the bishop vests in the sacristy; he does not take his vestments from the altar. *Ordo Romanus VI* in Migne, *P.L.* 78, 986.

toral staff. 3. Six subdeacons in tunicles followed by the canon-subdeacon. 4. Six deacons in dalmatics followed by the canon-deacon. 5. Six priests in chasubles. Finally comes the archbishop vested ready for Mass with two assistants in copes holding the gremial in front of him. Behind him walk two other chaplains and the archbishop's private chaplain, all in copes. The archbishop arrives at the altar, the acolytes put down their candles, the deacons and subdeacons and the assistant priests line up in their places. We may feel that we are back in the times of St Gregory the Great.[5]

After the preparatory prayers the archbishop goes to the throne (which is in the apse facing down the church) and it is there that he reads the introit, intones the *Gloria,* sings the collect, listens to the Epistle and Gospel.

During the Epistle the priest-sacristan of the cathedral puts on a cope and accompanied by subdeacons goes to prepare the *oblata.* At the end of the embolism to the Lord's Prayer (*Libera nos*—at Lyons this is always said aloud or sung) the archbishop gives a solemn blessing. First the canon-deacon raises the crozier, turns to the people and sings: *Humiliate vos ad benedictionem* ("Bow down for the blessing"), to which the

[5] Cf. W. Frere, *The Principles of Religious Ceremonial* (London, 1928), p. 59.

The seven representatives of each order have been accounted for by reference to the seven heavenly spirits and the golden candlesticks of the Apocalypse. A more probable explanation is that originally the fourteen districts of Rome had each, every other day, to provide one deacon, one subdeacon and one acolyte for the stational Mass. The six priests were introduced in France for the sake of symmetry: at Rome their number was unlimited, they assisted the pontiff and consecrated with him and other bishops who were present. Nowadays at Lyons the assistant priests consecrate with the bishop (that is, they concelebrate) on Maundy Thursday only, the sole vestige of this ancient rite anywhere in the West with the exception of the ordination Mass. Before the Revolution it was a common practice in the cathedrals of France. Cf. Amalarius, writing of Maundy Thursday: *Mos est romanae ecclesiae ut in confectione immolationis Christi adsint presbyteri et simul cum pontifice verbis et manibus conficiant.* (Migne, *P.L.* 105, 106.)

choir replies *Deo gratias,* the archbishop then gives the blessing according to the formula for the day. There are nineteen
of these each consisting of five clauses (the last two of which
are invariable). On Maundy Thursday and Easter day between
the first two petitions of the *Agnus Dei* there is sung the
ancient, *Venite, populi,* a hymn that has often been cited as
one of the former Gallican vestiges in the rite of Lyons. It is
nothing of the sort for it crops up all over the West and is
probably a chant for the fraction inserted before Pope Sergius'
institution of the *Agnus Dei* had taken place.

High Mass

High Mass sung by a priest is necessarily based on the
pontifical form. The diocesan ceremonial lays down the number of ministers to assist the celebrant on the different days of
the year. Thus on ferial days and the lesser feasts he should
have one acolyte in an alb and deacon and subdeacon, also in
albs only. On greater feast days each minister is provided with
an additional two in each order, while on the chief solemnities
of the year these assistants are increased to four and there is
an assistant priest in rochet and tippet at the book.

Colour sequence, etc.

The colour sequence is the same as that of the Roman rite
but ash colour is used for Lent. At high Mass, and optionally
at low Mass, a large form of corporal is used; the official diocesan ceremonial prescribes that it shall be twenty-one and a
half inches by forty-three. When the chalice is standing on it
the corporal is brought up from the back to cover it, thus
obviating the use of a pall.

The Ordo Missae

The *Ordo Missae* is substantially the Roman form with
certain peculiarities which can be briefly indicated. The
prayers at the foot of the altar differ from those of the Roman

Missal; there is no psalm said at this point, merely three versicles and responses: *Introibo ad altare Dei* with its usual response; *Pone, Domine, custodiam ori meo* ("Lord, set a guard on my mouth") with the response *Et ostium circumstantiae labiis meis* ("Post a sentry before my lips"); *Confitemini Domino quoniam bonus* ("Praise the Lord for he is good") with the response *Quoniam in saeculum misericordia ejus* ("For his mercy endures for ever"). The *Confiteor* follows the Roman form but there is a longer form of *Misereatur* said by the celebrant (it begins *Amen, fratres, per virtutem sanctae crucis...*). Then, after *Adjutorium nostrum* etc. and *Sit nomen Domini*, etc., with their responses, the celebrant goes up to the altar saying the prayer *Conscientias nostras*. On arrival at the altar he recites a long prayer *Deus qui non mortem*.

There are twenty sequences in the Lyons Missal; they must be sung at solemn Mass but are optional at low Mass, except for those in the Roman Missal. The short prayers and blessing of the deacon at the Gospel differ from those in the Roman Missal. At the offertory also the prayers are different. Uncovering the chalice the celebrant says the verse (in the Roman Missal it occurs before he receives communion from the chalice) *Quid retribuam Domino ... Calicem salutaris accipiam*, etc. Then follows a verse from St John's Gospel (6. 51) and after a sign of the cross over the host the celebrant at the Epistle corner pours wine into the chalice saying the prayer *De latere Domini nostri Jesu Christi* ("From the side of our Lord Jesus came forth blood [*here water is mixed with the wine*] and water at the time of his passion for the redemption of the world, that is, the mystery of the Holy Trinity; John the Evangelist saw it and gave testimony of it and we know that his testimony is true").[6] Host and chalice are offered together as the following prayer *Hanc oblationem* is said: "We

---

[6] Thus the present Missal. Cf. below, p. 65, the same prayer as said by the Carthusians who have preserved an earlier form.

pray you, Almighty God, to accept this oblation and to forgive the sins of all those offering it and of all those for whom it is offered to you." Then raising the vessels a little higher the celebrant says *In spiritu humilitatis*, etc. (slight verbal differences from the Roman form). Only two verses of Ps. 25 are said at the *Lavabo*. Returning to the middle of the altar he says the invocation of the Holy Spirit (*Veni, Sancte Spiritus* and the prayer *Suscipe sancta Trinitas*—a slightly expanded form). *Orate fratres* and its response also differ from those in the Roman rite.

There are seven proper prefaces in addition to those found in the Roman Missal (Advent, Maundy Thursday, St Pothinus and St Irenaeus, the Eucharist, St John the Baptist, All Saints and the Dedication of a Church). The canon textually is the same as that in the Roman Missal though some of the rubrics are different, the most striking being the direction after the consecration for the celebrant to extend his arms in the form of a cross.

The "little elevation" takes place during the Lord's Prayer at the words *sicut in caelo* when the celebrant, who has been holding the host over the chalice since the doxology, raises both so that they may be seen by the congregation. The *Libera nos* is sung or recited aloud as seems to have been the primitive Roman custom. The commixture is made after the *Agnus Dei* to the accompaniment of a prayer (*Haec sacrosancta commixtio*) that is to be found in many medieval rites and still in the Dominican *Ordo Missae*. The prayers at the communion and at the ablutions show certain differences.

THE RITE OF BRAGA

It has often happened in the past that a distinctive diocesan liturgy has perished through the difficulty and expense of reprinting the liturgical books for a relatively small number of clergy. The Roman books were always in plentiful supply and chapters and clergy have been prone to take the easier way out. Such a condition of affairs very nearly occurred in Braga, the archiepiscopal see in the North of Portugal, where by 1919 the majority of the clergy had abandoned their local rite. Their conduct may be condoned when it is remembered that the last edition of the Missal had been published in the sixteenth century.

Origins

Benedict XV declared the local rite to be obligatory for all the clergy of the diocese when the revised Breviary appeared in 1921. The new edition of the Missal was issued in 1924 and Pius XI in his letter of approbation speaks of the rite of Braga as *Lusitaniae nitidum velut speculum*. Both Benedict XV and Pius XI refer to the rite as dating from "remote times", though it is probably more accurate to say that like some other medieval variants of the Roman rite it belongs, at the earliest, to the twelfth century. Attempts to connect it with the Mozarabic rite and to seek its derivation therein have been made without success; in reality the time of its principal development belongs to the period of the Cluniac influence in the country. The Franco-Roman customs and the whole *ethos* of the rite show clearly that it is Roman with the addition of local customs, some of them of French origin, like many of the diocesan rites all over Europe before 1568.

During the seventeenth, eighteenth and nineteenth centuries sporadic attempts were made to achieve the reform of certain elements in the rite and to oppose the strong movement towards the Roman rite pure and simple. In fact, by the end of the nineteenth century, Braga was a diocese with two rites— that of Braga used in public while in private the clergy said the Roman Breviary and celebrated Mass in accordance with the rubrics of the Roman Missal.

When the fortunes of this diocesan liturgy had reached their lowest ebb at the turn of the century—by this time only a few churches in the diocese used the local rite—the reform of

Breviary and Missal was mooted and it seemed that the future might hold some promise of a revival, but the revolution of 1910 effectively postponed its achievement for a further few years. In 1916, however, the archbishop (Mgr Manuel Vieira de Mattos, 1915–32) entrusted Fr Antonio de Santa Maria, O.F.M., with the supervision of the printing in Rome of a new edition of the Missal and Breviary. The four volumes of the latter had all appeared by 1922 and the Missal in 1924; it was made obligatory in the diocese at once. The rubrics and calendar were adapted in conformity with those of the Roman Breviary and Missal then prevailing (that is, in accordance with the decree *Divino afflatu*) but the distinctive features of the rite were preserved. As with the other rites that are variants of the Roman (that is, those of the monastic Orders mentioned in the next chapter and that of Lyons) the reform of the Roman liturgy now in progress will doubtless cause further changes, but this is a necessary evolution, one that has occurred frequently in the past and will doubtless do so in the future.

The rite of Mass

The chalice is prepared before the beginning of low Mass and at the addition of the drops of water the prayer *Ex latere Domini nostri Jesu Christi* (cf. Lyons, Carthusians) is said, though in a version differing slightly from that in use elsewhere. At high Mass the chalice is prepared between the Epistle and Gospel. The prayers at the foot of the altar are almost the same as those in the Roman rite, but the *Confiteor* differs slightly. On important festivals the introit antiphon is repeated after the psalm verse as well as after the *Gloria Patri*. Since the revision of the Missal in 1924 the farcing of the *Gloria in excelsis* for feasts of our Lady has disappeared, some four hundred and fifty years after its abolition in the Roman rite. It was this farcing, common in the Middle Ages, that caused the insertion of the rubric in the Roman Missal (it remained down to 1912): *Sic dicitur* Gloria in excelsis *etiam in Missis beatae Mariae* ("The *Gloria in excelsis* is said thus even on feasts of Blessed Mary").[7]

At the offering of the host the prayer is: *Acceptabilis sit Majestati tuae*: "May this oblation be acceptable to your Majesty, Almighty God; we offer it for our sins and offences and for the good estate of the Catholic Church, as well as for all the faithful departed." The rest of the offertory prayers follow the Roman practice. The canon is identical with that of the Roman Missal. The prayers before the communion (there are four of them) are proper to Braga. There is an elevation before the communion. "And the priest turns his body slightly", says the rubric, "so that those nearby (*circumstantes*) may see the sacred host and adore it." The blessing at the end of Mass is in this form: *In unitate Sancti Spiritus benedicat vos Pater et Filius.* Mass concludes with a Marian antiphon and collect, a sixteenth-century introduction by Balthasar Limpo, a Carmelite archbishop of Braga.

It will be seen that in its present form the rite of Braga more nearly resembles the modern Roman rite than any of those, save that of the Premonstratensians, mentioned in this book. It may be worth mentioning that the Benedictine monks of Tibaes used a rite very similar to that of Braga and that this rite was used in Brazil as well as in Portugal until the beginning of the nineteenth century.

---

[7] Thus, *Qui tollis peccata mundi suscipe deprecationem nostram, ad Mariae gloriam ... Quoniam tu solus sanctus, Mariam sanctificans ...* etc.

CHAPTER IV

MONASTIC RITES

Diocesan liturgies by reason of their territorial restriction are not often encountered by the ordinary churchgoer; it is the rites of the religious Orders at which they are more likely to be present on occasion. Of the five examined in this chapter (those of the Carthusians, Cistercians, Premonstratensians, Carmelites and Dominicans) it is the last three that are the most widespread though it must be borne in mind that the Premonstratensians, Dominicans and Carmelites can muster between them only about 13,000 priests scattered throughout the world.

Although it is usually dangerous to generalize in these matters it can be stated that all the liturgies included in this chapter exhibit certain common characteristics, or at least did exhibit them at an early stage of their development. Thus on the question of origins it can be said that all these rites were derived from elements current in twelfth-century France. Most of the rites also have short preparatory prayers at the foot of the altar, prepare the chalice before Mass (at low Mass) or at the gradual (high Mass). Most of them, again, at the offertory call for host and chalice to be offered simultaneously. All, finally, show in many ways a greater simplicity than we are accustomed to in the Roman rite.

THE CARTHUSIAN RITE

Of all the rites in the West that survived the liturgical reform of the sixteenth century that of the Carthusians has preserved its primitive form better than any other. This may be accounted for by the fact of the Carthusians' living retired from the world and the healthy conservatism of a monastic Order devoted to solitude.

Origins

The Carthusian Mass is derived from the rite of the primatial see of Lyons (see above Chapter III) and is an example of that local influence which is continually to be found—we shall encounter it again with the Carmelite rite, for example—in any consideration of the origin of monastic liturgies. It must be borne in mind that with the Carthusians the influence of Lyons applies both to Office and Mass; while we are not here concerned with the Office it requires mentioning that Mass and Office together with the other rites make up the complete liturgy and that the Office and the evidence that it furnishes provide useful indications of origins. The first Carthusians looked to the Rule of St Benedict for the form of the Office and its general arrangement, but for the variable parts (apart from the distribution of the Psalms over the days of the week and the Hours of the Office) adopted local practice.

St Bruno founded his Order in a desert site called Chartreuse (*Cartusia*) in the diocese of Grenoble, a suffragan of Lyons; there seems little doubt that the first Carthusians adopted, in accordance with the custom of the times, the rite of the locality in which they found themselves. We have only to consider the many striking similarities between the Carthusian and Lyons rites to be convinced of this. The versicle with which the priest begins Mass (*Pone, Domine, custodiam ori meo*) the prayer said at the mingling of the drop of water with the already prepared wine (*De latere Domini nostri*, etc.) and lastly, the blessings of candles, ashes and palms; all these are common to both. Finally, in the ancient Carthusian manuscripts there is to be found an Office and Mass for the Octave day of Pentecost (since replaced by Trinity Sunday) and this too is to be found in the Lyons books; moreover, both count the Sundays between Pentecost and Advent from Trinity Sunday and are thus continually one behind the corresponding Sundays in the Roman rite; when they differ from the Roman rite they agree in the difference. The Roman rite ends the series with the Mass *Dicit Dominus,* while the Carthusians and the old Lyons books end it with *Si iniquitates.*

The actual compilation of the Missal was left to Guigues, the fifth prior of the Chartreuse. His *Consuetudines* is the oldest extant Carthusian document [1] of any interest from a liturgical point of view and a study of it is indispensable if we are to understand the early Carthusian liturgy. It appears that Guigues was much influenced by the principles of Agobard [2] who had laid down the principle that no uninspired compositions were to be used in the liturgy of the Church. Since then, of course, Agobard's principle has been largely discarded even at Lyons, but we find the whole question reopened in the seventeenth and eighteenth centuries, in France particularly, when many dioceses and religious Orders took it upon themselves to reform their Breviaries and Missals.

Happily Guigues did not follow Agobard to excess but the Carthusian rite still shows his influence. The details of the Mass, as given in the *Consuetudines,* are almost entirely identical with those of the Carthusian high Mass of today; very little has been changed or added. One or two details in which the early Carthusian Mass differed from its modern counterpart may be mentioned. Guigues calls for the use of the reed for the reception by the priest of the Precious Blood. Today this survives in the West only at a papal Mass. The deacon used to receive the Precious Blood when he communicated (the *Consuetudines* say that he is to do so on Sundays), but this was forbidden in the thirteenth century. This Sunday communion of the deacon is prescribed rather as an exception, and it seems

[1] It is reprinted in Migne, *P.L.* 153, 639.
[2] See above, p. 50.

that the rest of the community did not communicate more often than once a month. Moreover, the first Carthusians were not accustomed to daily Mass (it should be borne in mind that they were hermits as well as monks, and predominantly hermits) and the conventual Mass was celebrated only a few times in the week. The custom of the monthly general communion is still in force in the Charterhouses on the first Sunday of every month for all those not in Orders; and on the three chief solemnities of the year—Christmas, Easter and Whitsun—all the monks communicate at the high Mass sung by the prior.

Vestments

The vestments in use with the Carthusians are the same as those throughout the West, except that when the priest is seated he uses a gremial veil (cf. Carmelites, Dominicans); in the Roman rite this is reserved to a bishop. The stole is not crossed, but is left hanging loosely under the chasuble. The deacon is vested simply in the "church cowl" (*cuculla ecclesiastica*), a flowing garment much like a surplice, made of white wool. The stole which he puts on to sing the Gospel is worn over the left shoulder, wound round his body and brought under the right arm across the body so as to hang over the left arm like a maniple.[3] For the offertory he wears a *syndon* which is nothing else than a humeral veil worn over the left shoulder only, and left hanging loose; he uses this vestment also in moving the Blessed Sacrament and when he communicates. There is no subdeacon, and such vestments as the cope, the dalmatic and the tunicle are unknown among the Carthusians. For low Mass two candles are lighted and another at the elevation. At high Mass two are used on ordinary or ferial days and four to six on solemnities according to the custom of the house. Formerly there was but one light on the altar, enclosed

---

[3] In the *Consuetudines* we find: *Diaconus ponat stolam super humerum sinistrum et per dextrum latus receptam involvit pro manipulo in sinistra manu.*

in a lantern and a vestige of this practice is to be found in the Carthusian *Ordinarium* of 1869 which directs that on Candlemas day there shall be a light which may be so enclosed. The additional light at the elevation is still ordered in the Roman Missal but it has largely fallen into disuse. It has been retained by the Dominicans.

Carthusian Mass rite

The celebrant having vested goes to the deacon's lectern (halfway down the sanctuary and facing the Epistle side of the altar) and after making the sign of the cross with the usual words chants the versicle *Pone, Domine, custodiam ori meo* ("Lord, set a guard on my mouth") to which the whole choir replies *Et ostium circumstantiae labiis meis* ("Post a sentry before my lips"). The *Confiteor* [4] follows, then singing *Adjutorium nostrum*, etc. "Our help is in the name of the Lord," etc.) the celebrant goes to the altar steps and bowing profoundly says a *Pater* and *Ave*. The choir meanwhile begins the introit. The priest reads the introit, Kyrie and, if it is to be sung, intones the *Gloria*[5] at the Epistle corner. Here, too, he sings *Dominus vobiscum* and the collects. After the collects he goes to the *cathedra*, a chair opposite and facing the deacon's lectern, and sitting there listens to the Epistle, which is sung by a monk at the lectern in the choir. In monasteries of Carthusian nuns it is sung by one of the "consecrated" nuns in their choir.

[4] The form of the *Confiteor* is as follows: *Confiteor Deo omnipotenti et beatae Mariae et omnibus sanctis et vobis fratres quia peccavi nimis mea culpa per superbiam cogitatione locutione opere et omissione, precor vos orare pro me*. Notice that the *Confiteor* is not said in front of the altar, even at a low Mass: *Hanc vero confessionem facimus non ante altaris medium, sed ad sinistram ejus partem*. Thus the *Ordinarium*. This was the custom at Cluny and Westminster, for example, and may still be seen in the Roman rite at a low Mass said in the presence of a bishop.

[5] In the Carthusian Missal the following inversion occurs: *propter gloriam tuam magnam*.

The deacon meanwhile has been preparing the *Oblata* at the piscina unless the *Credo* is to be sung (infrequently apart from Sundays) and towards the end of the Alleluia or Tract comes to the celebrant to ask a blessing and be invested with the stole. The thurible is presented to the celebrant for incense to be put in; he does this without any formula or blessing. He stands at the *cathedra* for the singing of the Gospel and then returns to the middle of the altar where the book is brought for him to kiss. Then, if it is to be sung, he intones the *Credo* [6] and recites it while the choir sings it.

He goes to the Epistle corner for the *Lavabo* and receives the corporal from the deacon, spreads it open in the middle of the altar and going once more to the Epistle corner there receives the *Oblata* from the deacon who mingles a drop of water with the wine while the priest says the prayer *De latere Domini nostri Jesu Christi*, etc. ("From the side of our Lord Jesus Christ came forth blood and water for the remission of sins, in the name of the Father and of the Son and of the Holy Ghost"). Paten and chalice are offered together with a single prayer *In spiritu humilitatis,* identical in text with that to be found in the Roman rite after the offering of the chalice. The celebrant then censes the *Oblata* and the altar [7] and washes his hands for the second time. The deacon then censes the altar; to do so he walks round it swinging the thurible at the full length of its chains.

The canon is identical with that of the Roman Missal, save for one or two unimportant changes in the order of words. Right through the canon until the end of the *Libera nos* the celebrant stretches out his arms in the form of a cross unless he has some manual act to perform. He does not genuflect at the consecration but bows profoundly and there is no elevation

---

[6] In the Carthusian Missal the following conclusion occurs: *vitam futuri saeculi*. See *Facsimiles of the Creeds* (Henry Bradshaw Society, 1908), plates 12 and 13 with text on them.

[7] Note that in the Carthusian rite only things not persons are censed.

of the chalice. After the *Pax Domini* one petition of the *Agnus Dei* is said; the Pax is given with an *instrumentum pacis* or "Pax brede". Then after a prayer, *Domine Jesu Christe, Fili Dei vivi*, which is a slightly expanded form of the one in the Roman Missal, the celebrant communicates without pausing between the reception of the sacred species. If communion is given—the deacon is bound to communicate on Sundays with the priest—it is administered without any confession, form of absolution or *Domine non sum dignus*, but simply with the words *Corpus Domini nostri Jesu Christi custodiat te in vitam aeternam*. The communion finished, the choir sings the two remaining portions of the *Agnus Dei* and then the communion anthem. The celebrant takes the two ablutions and, having washed his hands, leaves the chalice midway between the book and the centre of the altar for the deacon to purify at the piscina while the *complendae* (or postcommunions) are being sung. After these prayers *Dominus vobiscum* is repeated and the deacon sings *Ite missa est* or *Benedicamus Domino* as required by the Office. Here the Carthusian Mass finishes and, if an Hour of the Office in choir follows immediately, the celebrant at once begins it by intoning its opening versicle (*Deus in adjutorium*, etc.); having said the *Placeat* (which is regarded as a private prayer) he then retires.

The ceremonies of low Mass are derived from those of high Mass and are, of course, a later development. The priest prepares the *Oblata* before the Mass and covers the chalice and paten with a pall, leaving them midway between the book and the centre of the altar. He reads the Mass as far as the Gospel at the Epistle corner, changing the book over himself for the Gospel. At the offertory he first of all mingles water with the wine and then washes his hands while saying some of the verses of Ps. 25. He then offers up paten and chalice together as at high Mass. From this point there is no difference in ceremonial from the usage at high Mass save that the priest himself purifies the chalice at the piscina after Mass is over.

The Proper of the Season

The Proper of the Season offers some points of interest. On Christmas Eve and at the three Masses of Christmas day there is a short lesson from Isaias read before the Epistle. The various blessings which occur during the course of the liturgical year (candles, ashes and palms) take place after the priest has said the *Confiteor* and gone up to the altar. On Candlemas day a single collect is used to bless the candles; during the distribution the usual antiphon (*Lumen ad revelationem*) is sung, and after the offertory anthem the candles are offered at the altar and received by the celebrant. The prayer used at the blessing of ashes is the same as that in the Lyons rite. The blessing of palms is analogous and there is no lesson or Gospel as in the Roman rite. The Carthusians have no liturgical processions.

In comparison with other rites of more or less medieval origin the Carthusian liturgy is remarkable for its simplicity, not only in its ceremonial but also in the liturgical forms themselves. If we compare it with the Sarum rite now obsolete or with the present-day Dominican rite this is seen to be very obvious: the one simple to a degree, with its plain though dignified Mass, entire absence of anything like liturgical splendour and its almost exclusive use of Scripture; the others with ornate ceremonial at Mass, popular sequences and rhyming responsories would seem to belong to a different age of liturgical development and not to practically the same period. Yet it is the Carthusian rite which portrays for us the essential simplicity of the Roman rite of which, through Lyons, it is an outgrowth.

THE CISTERCIAN RITE

Exceptionally here the ancient rite rather than modern Cistercian practice has been described in order to portray the

stage of liturgical evolution in the twelfth century and also
because a description of the modern Cistercian Mass would be
merely an account of the Mass of the Roman Missal with
which we are familiar. Save for certain features of the Proper
of the Season (the various blessings—candles, ashes, palms—
and some other ceremonies that occur in the course of the
year) the Cistercians follow the Roman *Ordo Missae* with the
addition of certain monastic practices. Towards the beginning
of the seventeenth century various General Chapters expressed
the wish to bring the liturgical books of the Order into agree-
ment with those of the Roman rite; a new Breviary (on the
monastic pattern) was published in 1608 and the Roman *Ordo
Missae* was adopted in 1618. Claude Vaussin, Abbot of
Cîteaux, published reformed books (in 1656 and 1657) which
were approved by Rome. This form of the old Cistercian rite,
modified to follow more closely the modern Roman rite, was
definitively approved in 1869 by the Congregation of Rites.

Origins

The Cistercians were in full possession of their ancient rite
in 1570 when Pius V published his reformed Roman Missal; it
is a pity that less than a hundred years later they abandoned
the greater part of their old usages for these crystallized practices that went back to the eleventh century and even earlier;
in the main, and leaving out of account more modern accre-
tions, infiltrations and unintelligent copying of later Roman
practices, they show us the Roman rite at different stages of its
development.

St Robert and the twenty-one monks who had left Molesmes
with him arrived at Cîteaux on March 21st, 1098, bringing
with them what was necessary for the celebration of Mass and
the Divine Office. In the subsequent dispute with the monks of
Molesmes those of Cîteaux were allowed by the papal legate,
Hugh, Archbishop of Lyons, to keep all save a *breviarium*

quoddam; this latter they might retain for copying until the feast of St John Baptist next following.[8]

We do not know what this *breviarium* contained. (It was certainly not a Breviary in the modern sense of the word.) A Cistercian authority[9] asserts that it was a compendium of liturgical texts, similar to that contained in the Dijon manuscript mentioned later, but he offers no evidence for this assertion. The other hypothesis is that it was a lectionary, and some support is lent to this alternative by the fact that the *breviarium* that forms a considerable part of the Dijon manuscript is a lectionary. Whatever St Robert's breviary contained, therefore, it is of little use now in determining the origins of the primitive Cistercian *Ordo Missae*.

We have the venerable authority of Cardinal Bona for the statement that the custom of the times would have required the first Cistercians to follow the local diocesan use. Cîteaux was situated in the diocese of Châlons-sur-Saône, in the ecclesiastical province of Lyons; on that score it seems likely that the early Cistercians, like the early Carthusians, adopted the local variant of the Roman rite in use in that province—though, unlike the Carthusians, they did not keep to it so faithfully nor for so long. Cluny and Molesmes very probably furnished certain elements, particularly as they too were in the province of Lyons.

With the establishment of Cîteaux on a firm basis and the foundation of its first daughter houses can be remarked the emergence of that principle of uniformity and centralization not only in government and religious observance but also in divine worship that marks off the Cistercians so clearly from the Black Monks—and the Premonstratensians (*sacer et candi-*

[8] *Exord. Cist. Coenobii.* Printed in *Les Monuments primitifs de la Règle Cistercienne publiés d'après les manuscrits de l'abbaye de Cîteaux par* Ph. Guignard (Dijon, 1878), p. 66. (Quoted hereafter as Guignard.)

[9] Dom André Malet, *La Liturgie Cistercienne* (Westmalle, 1921), p. 11.

dus Ordo) from the Black Canons. *Volumus,* says the *Carta Caritatis, ut mores et cantum et omnes libros ad horas diurnas et nocturnas et ad missas necessarios secundum formam morum et librorum novi monasterii possideant.*[10] We know that a reform was undertaken, but we know hardly anything of it concerning the Missal, merely the final result and not what was worked on nor what was produced in the intervening years. Principally it seems that this reform concerned the text rather than the rite, for in copying the Molesmes books the text was discovered to be corrupt and the first Cistercians were eager to use nothing but an authentic text.[11] St Stephen undertook the correction of the Bible, St Bernard the books of chant. The Metz antiphoner was copied; envoys were sent to Milan for the text of the hymns. The reform appears to have been complete by the time that the *Carta Caritatis* was drawn up, that is, by 1115–18.

Some sixty years later a definitive form was given to these earlier essays—changes were made perhaps in the light of experience—and Cistercian liturgical practice emerges almost mature. It is to be found in the manuscript (n. 114) of the Dijon municipal library, which belonged originally to Cîteaux and was intended as the *editio typica* of the Cistercian liturgical books by which all others were to be corrected, the standard to which in the interests of uniformity all others must conform. It was written between 1173 and 1191 and consists of fifteen parts: I–III *Breviarium* (i.e. lectionary for the Divine Office), IV *Epistolare*, V Gospel book, VI Missal, VII *Collectaneum*, VIII *Kalendarium*, IX *Regula* (of St Benedict), X *Consuetudines*, XI Psalter, XII *Cantica*, XIII Hymnal, XIV Antiphoner, XV Gradual. The frontispiece enumerating the contents of the book is bordered by a rubric pointing out very

[10] Guignard, p. 80.

[11] St Bernard: *Inter cetera quae optime aemulati sunt patres nostri ... hoc quoque studiosissime et religiosissime curaverunt, ut in divinis laudibus, id cantarent, quod magis authenticum inveniretur.* (*Opera omnia,* 1. 13.)

clearly the intended use of the book.[12] Unfortunately parts XI–XV are missing—they were abstracted *circa* 1480—and for the Mass we are left with the Missal and the *Consuetudines*.[13] But the Missal, it is worth pointing out, ought, properly speaking, to be described as a Sacramentary, for it contains only the celebrant's part of the Mass: *Ordo Missae*, collects, secrets, postcommunions; the celebrant of a high Mass did not in those days say everything that was sung by choir or ministers, and consequently had no need of introits, Epistles, Gospels, etc., in his book.

There can be distinguished, then, three periods in the establishment of the Cistercian liturgy: first, the books and customs brought from Molesmes, second, the reform of this liturgy effected by 1115–18 when its use was prescribed by the *Carta Caritatis*, third, the final form as it emerges some sixty years later (1173 at the earliest) in the Dijon manuscript.

If, as I have said, local influence was paramount in the early Cistercian *Ordo Missae*, we must still reckon with other elements. The compiler of the *Consuetudines* seems to have had two principles in mind. The first, and this is particularly noticeable, is a desire above all for simplicity. Compare the *Consuetudines* with, for example, the early Premonstratensian *Ordinarium* of a few years earlier (which derives to some extent from previous Cistercian redaction), and this stands out very clearly. The other characteristic is a care for authentic

[12] Guignard, viii (Frontispiece in colour facing title page). The inscription reads: *In hoc volumine continentur libri ad divinum officium pertinentes quos utique non decet in ordine nostro diversos haberi. Sunt autem in unum corpus ea maxime redacti ut presens liber sit exemplar invariabile ad conservandam uniformitatem et corrigendam in aliis diversitatem.*

[13] The *Consuetudines* are in Guignard, pp. 87–287, but not the *Missale*: probably it is for this reason that Dom Trilhe does not do more than mention its existence in his article on the Cistercian rite in DACL III, 1779–1811. The *Ordo Missae* from the *Missale* has been reprinted in *Collectanea* O.C.R. VI, 1 (April 1939), pp. 40–3. That part of *Consuetudines* referring to the ceremonies of Mass occurs in Guignard on pp. 141–61.

primitive, Roman practice, a certain respect for the *Ordines Romani*, even though the best Roman models were not then to be found in Rome but in the Rhineland. It is true that the Cistercian compiler seems sometimes to misunderstand the *Ordines*, but he realized their importance for his purpose. Are there any other sources? Cluny is obvious and has been mentioned already, although the Cistercian compiler allowed his desire for simplicity full scope. Cluny's influence is important; it was widespread, reaching even to the primatial church of Lyons, and it provides the connecting link with what was then possibly the predominating liturgical influence of the West, Lotharingia, the Pontifical of Mainz and the later *Ordines Romani*.

What follows here is a summary reconstruction of the early Cistercian Mass with some reference to later additions. Certain parts are treated in greater detail because they show certain affinities to the sources which I have suggested.[14]

The Ordo Missae

The deacon and subdeacon, vested in amice, alb, girdle and maniple, went from the sacristy to prepare the altar and spread the altar cloths; the Gospel book was placed on its lectern, and the Missal at the Epistle side of the altar. Together with the celebrant they were present at Terce, and then returned with him to the sacristy for their remaining vestments.[15] When all were vested they washed their hands;[16] in the meantime,

---

[14] There is a short description by Dom Trilhe in the article in DACL already referred to. A detailed description of the Cistercian Mass according to the *Consuetudines* and the later manuscript and printed Missals is provided by Fulgence Schneider, O.C.R., *L'Ancienne Messe Cistercienne* (Tilburg, 1929). I disagree with many of his conclusions (particularly on the subject of the influence of the "Greek" rite) but have followed him for the contents of printed Missals. He does not appear to have consulted the Dijon prototype Missal.

[15] Or after the *Sub tuum* and collect *Pietate* chanted by the celebrant before the altar, a practice introduced in 1553.

[16] Cf. the practice at Cluny (Migne, *P.L.* 149, 715 and 724).

directly after Terce, two candles were lighted and the cantor began the introit. The celebrant with his ministers proceeded to the choir but stood for a moment at the "altar of the station"—at Cîteaux in the east transept—until the *Gloria Patri*; thereupon they bowed profoundly and went through the choir and up to the sanctuary. After another profound bow the celebrant went up to the altar, where bowing low again he said secretly the anthem *Veni sancte Spiritus,* then, kissing the altar, *In nomine Patris,* etc. The deacon now went to kiss the altar, and both came down together for the *Confiteor,* etc. When this was said, and after the versicle *Adjutorium,* etc., the ministers went to the credence table and the celebrant went to the altar saying secretly *Pater, Ave, Aufer a nobis.*[17]

That is the order in the later Missals. The *Consuetudines,* with an eye it seems on the Roman *Ordines,* arranged things differently in some cases. The *Ordines* mention the reverence to the altar at the first station; the *Consuetudines* make it the altar in the transept as above. According to the *Ordines,* the priest prays on arrival at the altar, and so tradition has evolved the *Confiteor* at this point; the *Ordo Missae* in the Dijon manuscript calls here for *Pater* and *Aufer a nobis,* afterwards the *Confiteor* as well. In the *Consuetudines* the celebrant is to kiss the altar before the deacon, in the *Ordines* it was the other way round. A comparison along these lines could be made at almost all points in the Mass, and in general would support my assertion that the Cistercian compiler tried to follow the *Ordines* though sometimes he misunderstood them. Such a comparison cannot be made here if this description is to be kept within bounds. A rubric in the *Consuetudines* that reads strangely to modern ears is that which directs the saying of the *Confiteor* at some later convenient moment if

[17] The form of *Confiteor* was: *Confiteor Deo et beatae Mariae et amnibus sanctis et vobis fratres quia peccavi nimis cogitatione, locutione et opere mea culpa. Ideo precor vos, orate pro me.* This form of *Confiteor* is of Cluniac origin. The Cistercians added *beatae Mariae* by order of the general chapter of 1184.

there was not time for it on arrival at the altar;[18] the principle
in those days was that the celebrant must not keep the choir
waiting, so after a short introit and simple Kyrie he might have
to intone the *Gloria* or sing *Dominus vobiscum* and be unable
to say the *Confiteor*, the completion of his private preparation,
until later (e.g. during the Epistle). There was no incensing at
the introit.

When the celebrant had gone up to the altar, the deacon and
subdeacon set about preparing the *oblata*. The subdeacon is
directed first of all to wash out the chalice with water. If during this time the *Gloria* was intoned or the collect sung, the
ministers were directed to leave what they were doing and
stand behind the priest, returning afterwards (while the choir
sang the *Gloria* or during the second collect) to the credence.
After the celebrant had added the drop of water to the chalice
it was put back on the credence in readiness for the offertory.

The celebrant intoned the *Gloria* at the Epistle corner and
there, too, he turned for the *Dominus vobiscum* and sang the
collects. After the collects, when the subdeacon went to sing
the Epistle, the celebrant could go and sit in the special stalls
near the altar. After the Epistle the subdeacon could return to
the altar, or, if the priest were sitting, to the stalls by the altar,
or, if need be, he could go to the choir to help with the singing—a practical point in a small community. The *Consuetudines* say that during the Epistle and gradual the priest could
read in the Missal,[19] a reference probably to the lengthy *Apolo-
giae* provided for this purpose (before the *Ordo Missae* in the
Dijon manuscript is the so-called "prayer of St Ambrose"
Summe sacerdos). The deacon was at liberty to look over the
Gospel he was about to sing, sitting at the stall by the celebrant's side or, if the latter remained standing at the altar, he
could go to the Gospel lectern for this purpose.

[18] *Consuetudines*: *Quam confessionem, si ea hora complere non
potuerunt, dicant postea, cum eis vacuum fuerit.* Guignard, p. 142.
[19] *Interim sacerdos usque ad evangelium sedere et in missali legere
potest.* Guignard, p. 143.

The celebrant carried the Missal back to the altar and remained there at the Epistle side during the singing of the Gospel. The deacon asked a blessing of the abbot if he were present, otherwise of the celebrant, before singing the Gospel. If the *Credo* was to be sung it was intoned from the Epistle side,[20] and there the celebrant remained until it was time to sing *Dominus vobiscum* and *Oremus,* the deacon and subdeacon standing behind him. He then picked up the Missal and carried it to the other side. The deacon unfolded the corporal (it was considerably larger than our modern ones) and going to the credence brought back the paten and chalice to the altar. The celebrant placed the paten on the chalice and holding them up said the offertory prayer—one form for both bread and wine: *Suscipe sancta Trinitas.* Some of the later Missals prescribe that it should be said kneeling—surely an anomaly: *elevans calicem et genua flectens dicat Suscipe.* Is such a practice to be found elsewhere? A Cistercian author says of the Spanish congregation that the celebrant recited the offertory prayer standing, and that this was done owing to the influence of the Roman rite after the splitting up of the Order into congregations. The use of the prayer *Suscipe* is at all events a later addition and neither the *Consuetudines* nor the Dijon prototype mention it. Presumably the obligatory accompaniment of every ritual act by a form of secret prayer was not then universal. The chalice was then placed on the corporal by the deacon with the host in front, a departure from the common medieval practice which was to place them side by side.[21] The part of the corporal behind the chalice was brought up and over it, thus serving as a pall.

[20] The *Credo* concluded with . . . *vitam futuri saeculi.* Cf. Carthusian rite. See *Facsimiles of the Creeds,* plates XII and XIII and text on them (Henry Bradshaw Society, 1908).

[21] Cf. *Micrologus* (Gerbert, O.S.B., *Monumenta veteris Liturgiae alemannicae,* II, 330): *Ita autem juxta Romanum ordinem in altari componenda sunt, ut oblata in corporali posita, calix ad dextrum latus oblatae ponatur, quasi sanguinem Domini suscepturus, quem de latere Dominico profluisse credimus.*

Oblata and altar were now incensed. Up till this moment, except at the time of vesting, the *Consuetudines* mention no acolyte or other minister except deacon and subdeacon. One now makes his appearance abruptly—*unus ministrorum cujus officium est*—who takes the thurible to the abbot (in his absence the celebrant) for it to be blessed, the subdeacon carrying the boat. The celebrant censed the *oblata* by making a circle around them with the thurible—that was all—and then, from the same position, censed the altar by one swing to the left, one to the right and one in the centre.[22] The deacon now censed the Epistle corner and the cross in the centre with a double swing, and passing round behind the altar came to the Gospel corner which he censed in like manner; he also censed the cross. Meanwhile the celebrant washed his hands, and coming back to the centre of the altar, bowing down, said the prayer *In spiritu humilitatis,* kissed the altar and turned round to say *Orate fratres*; to this the answer was: *Dominus sit in corde tuo et in labiis tuis suscipiatque de manibus tuis sacrificium istud et orationes tuae ascendant in memoriam ante Deum pro nostra et totius populi salute.*[23]

At *per omnia saecula saeculorum* after the secret prayer (which was said at the Gospel corner) the subdeacon took the offertory veil, enveloped the paten and went to stand in his place; he was directed to sign himself with the paten at the *Sanctus.*

There is little to detain us in the canon. The *Consuetudines*[24] speak neither of elevation nor of reverence at the consecration. Choir (*versis vultibus ad altare*) and ministers stood until the end of the canon.[25] The elevation of the host was ordered

[22] *Consuetudines,* Guignard, p. 144.

[23] Schneider says (*op. cit.,* p. 153) that there was no answer to the *Orate fratres* in the early Missals (as nowadays in the Dominican Missal). That given here occurs, however, in the Dijon prototype.

[24] Guignard, p. 146.

[25] The elevation of the host dates from the end of the twelfth century. It is ordered in the Carthusian Statutes of Jancelin, *c.* 1222.

by the general chapter in 1210, and the ringing of a bell at this moment only in 1601. The elevation of the chalice was also a later development; it was ordered by Eugenius IV in 1437 for the Cistercians of the Spanish congregation, and in 1444 by the General Chapter for the whole Order. The genuflection was a much more recent addition, even as late as the seventeenth century. The *Unde et memores* was said with arms outstretched in the form of a cross until the manual acts. An attentive reading of the *Consuetudines* shows that at the time of its composition all the emphasis was on the "little elevation", not on the consecration. When the deacon saw the celebrant signing the chalice (at *sanctificas, vivificas*) he was to go up to the celebrant's right hand, kiss the altar and make ready to uncover the chalice (*componat se honeste ad discooperiendum calicem*).[26] With his right hand he took hold of the corporal covering the chalice, while the priest did so on the other side with his left; together they folded it back. Then the celebrant, as he said *omnis honor et gloria,* holding the host over the chalice, lifted the latter in his left hand while the deacon aided him with his right; in this position *per omnia saecula saeculorum* was sung. After *Amen,* and when he had sung *Oremus,* the celebrant replaced the chalice and the host on the corporal, and with the deacon's help covered the chalice as before.

The Cistercian Mass (in common with others in the Middle Ages) was interrupted after the *Pater noster* for various suffrages prescribed by papal or capitular authority. Thus in 1213 Innocent III ordered Ps. 78 (*Deus venerunt gentes*) with a collect to be sung after the *Pater*[27]; the Cistercians already did

When two Masses were said *in conventu* the early Cistercians could remain sitting at the *missa matutinalis* from the *Sanctus* onwards: *Ad missam matutinalem ... sedeat qui voluerit ... post sanctus usque ad finem misse preter Agnus dei,* Guignard, p. 153.

[26] Guignard, p. 146.

[27] The decree may be seen in Migne, *P.L.* 216, 821. The Carmelites and Carthusians retained this practice down to fairly recent times.

so by order of their general chapter of 1194, repeated in 1196 and 1197. In 1245 the Crusade then in preparation was the cause of another decree to the same effect, repeated in 1261, but for a different intention; this time it was to ask God to avert the Tartar invasion (*cum tuba praeconii terribilis nostris intonuerit auribus super ingruenti saevitia Tartarorum, qui, sicut dicitur, sibi subjugare intendunt universum populum Christianum . . .*).[28] In 1302 the psalm *Deus misereatur* was ordered, and in 1328 John XXII ordered the psalm *Laetatus sum* as a suffrage from the whole Church for the pope in his difficulties. In the Cistercian Missal these various suffrages eventually evolved into the daily recital of the psalm *Laetatus sum* and collect after the *Pater noster*. When the Roman rite was adopted the suffrage disappeared, but the Cistercians have kept the practice of singing the *O salutaris hostia* immediately after the consecration; it was introduced originally by Dom Nicholas Boucherat, Abbot of Cîteaux, in 1574. With such practices we are in a very different world from that of the *Consuetudines*. Another interruption occurred after the abbots had received the use of pontificalia: at the end of the *Libera nos* they gave the solemn blessing when they sang Mass. Neither blessing nor suffrages are mentioned in the *Consuetudines*, but the solemn blessing at this point in the Mass is of course common in the Gallican Massbooks and it has been kept in the Lyons Missal and by the diocese of Autun.

As the celebrant said the conclusion of the *Libera nos* he broke the host lengthwise into three equal portions over the chalice; then, holding two of the particles in his left hand, with one in his right hand he made three signs of the cross within the chalice as he sang *Pax Domini,* etc.[29] He then placed this particle in the chalice saying *Haec sacrosancta commixtio,* etc. The *Agnus Dei* was said before this prayer. Still holding the two remaining particles in his left hand, he gave the kiss of

[28] Schneider, *op. cit.,* p. 179.
[29] *Consuetudines,* Guignard, p. 147.

peace to the deacon,[30] who passed it to the subdeacon and he in his turn to those who were to communicate. Then, placing one particle on the paten and holding the other (now in both hands) over the chalice, the celebrant said the prayer *Domine Jesu Christe, Fili Dei vivi,* etc. Directly he had said this prayer he communicated with the particle of the host he was holding, and then (without pause) from the chalice. No other prayer is mentioned at this point.

It was the custom for the ministers to communicate at the conventual Mass, even on Good Friday, but not at Masses for the Dead. The celebrant broke the remaining portion of the host into two over the paten, and communicated the deacon and the subdeacon (no formula is mentioned in the *Consuetudines*). When the deacon rose from his knees to give place to the subdeacon he went to the chalice and, at a sign from the celebrant, communicated from it and then carried it to the subdeacon. If there were any other communicants they received the host from the priest at the altar and the Precious Blood through a reed of silver or silver gilt from the chalice held at the Gospel corner by the deacon. It is difficult to determine whether a ministerial chalice was used; it seems to be precluded by what is said of the communion in the *Consuetudines,* but later on, in reference to the ablutions, chalices (in the plural) are mentioned; and during the communion the deacon is directed to add wine to the consecrated wine in the chalice when necessary (this last practice is usually associated with the use of a ministerial chalice, but it is not conclusive evidence). Communion under both kinds for the deacon and the subdeacon lasted until 1437; the chalice was forbidden to other communicants by the general chapter in 1261.

The use of the reed (*fistula*) is described in detail in the *Consuetudines*—it probably went out of use after 1261—and the

[30] An operation that required some care, the host being in his hand. The *Consuetudines* expresses it succinctly: *Divertat os suum ad diaconum osculans illum.* Guignard, p. 147.

subdeacon is directed to hold it before him until the end of Mass; it must have been somewhat awkward when he was helping the deacon at the altar. It has been suggested that the use of the word *fistula* instead of *pugillaris*, etc., is evidence of a certain following of *Ordo Romanus* VI.

After the communion the celebrant, at the middle of the altar, purified his fingers over the chalice with wine ministered by the subdeacon; he then went to the piscina to wash his hands, and returning to the altar took two ablutions of wine from the chalice; leaving it on the corporal, he went to the Epistle corner to sing the postcommunion. The *Consuetudines* point out carefully that he is to leave the chalice standing upright and not to lay it down on its side.[31] Except during the first postcommunion or when he is singing *Ite missa est* or *Benedicamus Domino* the deacon, aided by the subdeacon, still encumbered with the reed, is occupied in folding the corporal and taking the chalice and paten to the credence for final purification. This was a lengthy rite. It involved purification of the reed and paten over the chalice and of the chalice itself, and might amount to as many as four ablutions. The deacon was directed to drink the first two and the subdeacon any others.

The Mass concluded with *Ite missa est* or *Benedicamus Domino*. The blessing and last Gospel were late (possibly sixteenth century) introductions. A general chapter of the sixteenth century laid down that the celebrant was to say the beginning of the Gospel of St John before he took off his alb.

After *Ite missa est* the celebrant said the prayer *Placeat* bowing low and then, kissing the altar, a further prayer, *Meritis et precibus* ("By the merits and prayers of these saints and of all his saints may the Almighty Lord have mercy upon us"). Making the sign of the cross he bowed profoundly and went to

---

[31] *Ponat (calicem) non reclinatum super altare.* Guignard, p. 149. Carthusian rubrics required the exact contrary: ... *Calix ... reversatur super patenam.* Martène, *De Antiquis Ecclesiae Ritibus* (Antwerp, 1736), Vol. I, 634–5.

the sacristy, alone if the deacon and subdeacon had not yet completed the purification of the vessels.

That was the rite on all days of twelve lessons. On days of lesser importance there is provision in the *Consuetudines* for the celebrant of the conventual Mass to be assisted by one minister who carried out, so far as the sacred orders he had received entitled him to do so, all the functions of deacon and subdeacon. If he were not in deacon's orders, the celebrant sang the Gospel and administered the chalice.

An attempt to revive the primitive Cistercian rite is at present being made, with the necessary authorization, at three houses of the Order—at Bocquen in Brittany, Poblet in Catalonia and Hauterive in Switzerland, though Bocquen is the only place where the old rite, as it had developed by the sixteenth century, is used daily both for Mass and Office. It is too early yet to say what the final result will be—whether, for example, the whole Cistercian Order will return to the ancient rite or at least to its *Ordo Missae*. In the present climate of liturgical reform, when the general trend is towards simplicity, such a return is not out of the question.

THE PREMONSTRATENSIAN RITE

As with the Cistercians, the Mass rite of the Premonstratensian Canons Regular was largely adapted in the seventeenth century to the Roman *Ordo Missae* of the Missal of St Pius V. As a result there is not very much to indicate in the way of present practices which differ from those of the ordinary Roman rite.

Origins and history

Cardinal Bona, the seventeenth-century Cistercian liturgist, says of the Premonstratensian Breviary: "It is generally thought that the Breviary of the Canons of Prémontré is no other than the ancient Roman Breviary that they have preserved in all its purity since they did not admit the changes and reforms that the popes have inserted in the Roman Breviary" (*De divina psalmodia* 18, 6). This remark might well be applied to the Premonstratensian Missal at the period shortly before that at which Cardinal Bona wrote.

St Norbert founded his Order in 1120 at Prémontré (*praemonstratus* or *pratum monstratum,* a clearing in the forest of Coucy in the diocese of Laon). For an Order of Canons Regular the liturgy is of prime importance and St Norbert's undertaking, since it was a reform of the Canons Regular, just as in effect the Cistercians were a reform of the Benedictines, seems to emphasize that particular facet of the canonical life. We do not know what were the liturgical prescriptions of the first Premonstratensians. It has been said that they adopted the usages of the Church of Laon but there is no evidence of this whatever and all the indications seem to show that on the contrary they followed the custom of the other Canons Regular of the period and the locality. The increase in the number of houses and the Cistercian-inspired form of government very early called for a great measure of uniformity in liturgical observance among the Premonstratensians.

The Mass rite, it seems clear, is derived from the recension of the Roman rite that developed on the Rhine and was imposed on Carolingian countries by Charlemagne, finally making its way to Rome itself where it was not without influence on local usages in the capital of Christendom itself. That, at any rate, was the framework. Elements were borrowed from other rites that had developed from the same source, from that of the Cluniacs and especially from the Cistercian rite. But there are also elements of the Premonstratensian rite which seem to be taken from that of the Canons Regular of the Holy Sepulchre (extended reference is made to the Holy Sepulchre rite in connection with the Carmelite liturgy below). Put very shortly the Premonstratensian Mass rite was derived from usages in vogue in France in the twelfth century and thus it shows certain affinities, or did so before the seventeenth century, with the other rites of this period studied in this book.

A first codification of the usages of the Order took place in the twelfth century and these *Consuetudines*, as they were called, were revised in the first half of the thirteenth century (between 1236 and 1245). Substantially these enactments continued in use down to the appearance of the Roman books of the Pian reform (1568 and 1570).

The books of the Order were reformed in accordance with the revised Roman books and the Missal resulting from this step appeared in 1622. It contained the *Ordo Missae* of the Roman Missal. Fewer changes were made in the Proper of the Season or the Proper of the Saints, but the votive Masses and other special Premonstratensian features suffered curtailment. In 1660 the general chapter ordered the suppression of all the sequences (save the Christmas *Laetabundus*) not to be found in the Missal of St Pius V.

Right at the end of the eighteenth century an attempt was made to revise (or rather recast) the books of the Order on the lines of the neo-Gallican Parisian liturgy of Charles de Vintimille which had appeared some fifty years earlier. Jean-Baptiste l'Écuy, the last abbot of Prémontré, endeavoured to make all the houses of the Order accept these new books. The Missal appeared in 1787 and was accepted by the French houses but by no others. In any case, it enjoyed a short-lived notoriety for all the French houses were swept away a few years later by the Revolution and many of those in other parts of Europe by the disturbances and wars which followed.

Ordo Missae

As a result of the adoption of the order of Mass from the Pian Roman Missal the chief differences to be described are ceremonial. At a high Mass the Gospel book is carried in during the entrance rite and is given to the celebrant to kiss before he goes up to the altar. Incensing of the altar at the introit takes place only on the more important feasts. The acolytes go to the sacristy during the conclusion of the *Gloria* to fetch the chalice and cruets which are carried into the church during the singing of the collect. The deacon then (or during the gradual, as convenient) unfolds the corporal. On feasts during the singing of the creed the members of the choir kiss the closed Gospel book taken round by the subdeacon saying to each *Haec est lex Christi* ("This is the law of Christ") to which is the answer *Corde credo et ore confiteor* ("I believe in my heart and profess it with my lips"). The genuflection at the creed is made from *Et incarnatus est* down to *Et resurrexit* exclusively. The addition of the word *hoc* (that is, *hoc sacrificium*) at the answer to the *Orate fratres* forms one of the few textual differences between the Premonstratensian and Roman *Ordo Missae*. During the conclusion of the secret the deacon takes the paten from the altar and raises it aloft in his right hand. It is then given to the subdeacon who wraps it in the humeral veil. During the preface the deacon is directed to cense towards the altar (three times to the right and three to the left) and then to walk round the altar, censing it as he goes.

At the beginning of the Lord's Prayer the deacon receives the paten from the subdeacon and holds it aloft from *Panem nostrum quotidianum* until the end of the prayer. This is the sole survival of an invitation to communion common in the Middle Ages. Otherwise the ceremonies of high Mass are those of the Roman rite.

The liturgical year

At the Mass of Christmas Eve and at the three Masses of Christmas day a prophetical lesson from Isaias is said before the Epistle. On Christmas day the sequence *Laetabundus* is sung. There are certain variations from the Roman rite in the ceremonies of the liturgical year (blessing of ashes, palms,

Holy Week) and the basis of the sanctoral shows affinities with
that of the Dominicans.

THE CARMELITE RITE

Origins and history

Wherever the truth lies in the much debated question of the
origin of the Carmelite Order we know at least that the Carmelites migrated to Europe in the first half of the thirteenth
century, that they were hermits and that they followed a Latin
liturgy based on that of the Canons of the Holy Sepulchre in
Jerusalem, a foundation made by Godfrey de Bouillon, king
of the ill-fated and short-lived Christian kingdom of Jerusalem. In the primitive rule given to the Carmelites by Albert,
patriarch of Jerusalem (it was confirmed by Honorius III in
1226), we find that those who could read were to say the psalms
at the various Hours as they were appointed by the institution
of the holy Fathers and the approved custom of the Church.
There is no doubt that the approved custom of the Church
means here the rite of the province of Jerusalem, the metro-
politan church of which was the Holy Sepulchre. Another
passage of the rule informs us that the first Carmelites kept to
their cells or near them throughout the day, only meeting together for Mass in the mornings.[32]

The rite of the Holy Sepulchre was founded chiefly on that
of Paris with an admixture of various elements from other
French dioceses. A comparison of the rite of Paris as it was
described by John Beleth [33] with the rite of the Holy Sepulchre
shows its close affinity with Parisian usages. To these however

[32] *Oratorium prout commodius fieri poterit construatur in medio
cellularum, ubi mane per singulos dies ad audienda missarum con-
venire debeatis, ubi hoc commode fieri potest.*

[33] Migne, *P.L.* 202, 14 *et seq.* The *Ordinarium* of the rite of the
Holy Sepulchre is to be found in MS. Lat. Barberini 659 in the Vatican
Library. A description and transcription of a considerable part of this
manuscript will be found in *Analecta Ord. Carmelitarum* I, 95 *et seq.*
(Rome, 1909).

were added certain local peculiarities such as processions for Christmas, Easter and the Ascension which, had, so to say, a topographical relevance in the Holy Land. Then there was the emphasis on the resurrection, the weekly commemoration of this mystery with a special high Mass on Sundays and so on.

This then was the liturgy brought by the Carmelites to Europe. Obviously they could not celebrate it with the magnificence required by the *Ordinale* of the Canons of the Holy Sepulchre for they were poor and few in number. The migration to Europe caused, we know, a change in the whole constitution of these hermits from the Holy Land; from being a small local congregation of hermits they developed within a short space of time into an international Order of mendicant friars. The beginning of this transformation occurred in about 1247 when the Rule was revised by two Dominicans. At the general chapter held at Messina in 1259 decrees about liturgical observance were made but unfortunately the *Acta* of this chapter have been lost. A Carmelite *Ordinale* of about this date or very shortly afterwards, discovered at Trinity College, Dublin, in the early part of this century, shows that considerable changes were made in the rite of the Holy Sepulchre and comparison between this *Ordinale* and that of the Dominicans of 1256 betrays a striking similarity. It is not surprising that the Carmelites should have followed Dominican usage. On coming to Europe from the Holy Land they found the Dominicans already well established; it was Dominicans who adapted the Carmelite Rule to conditions in Europe and the influence and prestige of the Dominican Order were at their height in the second half of the thirteenth century. Nor were the Carmelites the only ones to be influenced very strongly in the liturgical sphere by the Dominicans at this time.[34]

For a period, perhaps for half a century or more, the Carmelites appear to have used a rite that was largely Dominican. This *Ordinale* remained in force until 1312 when a new one

---

[34] The Crosier Canons are a case in point.

was approved at the general chapter held in London that year. This *Ordinale,* which is the fundamental document of the Carmelite rite, was the work of Sibert de Beka, later provincial of Germany. His object was to restore the Holy Sepulchre rite to the Carmelites, as the title of his work clearly shows: *Ordinale Fratrum Ordinis beatae Mariae de Monte Carmeli extractum et exceptum de approbato usu Dominici Sepulchri Ierosolymitanae ecclesiae in cuius finibus dictorum fratrum religio sumpsit exordium.*[35]

Sibert's *Ordinale* is still the basis of the Carmelite liturgy and it is noteworthy because it restored as far as possible those elements of the Holy Sepulchre rite which had disappeared from the earlier Dominican recension. In comparison with other contemporary liturgical documents it is much fuller and detailed; its importance as the chief Carmelite liturgical source can therefore be appreciated.

The points of similarity with the Holy Sepulchre rite may be briefly noticed. The introit antiphon was said three times on the principal festivals, before and after the psalm and after the *Gloria Patri*; on certain days there were two lessons before the Gospel, one prophetical and the other the Epistle; a solemn commemoration of the Resurrection was held on the Sunday next before Advent; except on the Sunday after the Ascension and Whitsunday and its octave day a high Mass of the resurrection was sung after Terce, while the proper Sunday Mass was said earlier in the day. Certain feasts in the calendar were also taken from the Holy Sepulchre rite (e.g. SS. Simeon, Alexander, Quiriacus, etc.).

The principal characteristic of Sibert de Beka's *Ordinale* was a certain simplicity combined, says Fr Benedict Zimmerman, with an archaic flavour, so that the Carmelite liturgy in

[35] An edition of Sibert de Beka's *Ordinale* was published (from MS. 193 in Lambeth Palace Library) by the late Fr Benedict Zimmerman, O.C.D.: *Ordinaire de l'Ordre de Notre-Dame du Mont Carmel* (Paris, 1910).

his view comes about midway between the Dominican and Carthusian rites.

In the course of the Middle Ages no changes of importance occurred beyond those common to all rites during that period: the multiplication of festal offices to the detriment of the celebration of the temporal cycle. An edition of the *Ordinale* was published in 1544, and all houses of the Order were expected to possess a copy. This edition repeated the rubric about sequences from Sibert de Beka's edition—like most others at the time the Carmelite rite possessed a great number—but the Missal, published three years previously, was without them all save five[36] on the orders of the General, Nicholas Audet. The Missal of 1574 was the first to prescribe a colour sequence.

This Missal of 1574 had been reformed, that is, as a consequence of the reform of the Roman rite, it was endowed with a new calendar and certain elements from the Roman Missal were admitted. A further edition appeared in 1578 with additional changes in the same direction. But several feasts of saints of the Order (or reputed to be of the Order) were omitted from the calendar which caused, it appears, general dissatisfaction. A new calendar was authorized in a brief of 1602 and came into use in 1610.[37]

A quarter of a century previously the Discalced Carmelites discarded their own rite to adopt the Roman. They did so, at the prompting of Nicholas Doria, their General, in order to demonstrate more clearly their complete separation from the parent branch of the Order. St Teresa all her religious life used

---

[36] The five were: Easter, Ascension (*Rex omnipotens die hodierna*), Whitsun (*Sancti Spiritus adsit nobis gratia*), Corpus Christi and in Masses for the Dead.

[37] The feasts in question were: SS. Denis, Peter Thomas, Andrew Corsini, Euphrosyna, Avertanus, Berthold, Albert, Simon Stock, Brocard, Gerard, Serapion, Spiridion. Some of them, by no stretch of the imagination, could be called Carmelites and of one, at least, there are the gravest doubts about her existence.

the Carmelite rite: she died four years before the reformed branch that she had founded abandoned the old rite. Fr Benedict Zimmerman writes: "Claiming that so many revisions had been made in the course of half a century that it was no longer possible to know what was the rite of the Holy Sepulchre, Nicholas Doria forced the province to give it up and adopt the Roman liturgy: the acts of the definitory (August, 1586) make no secret of the motive for this move which was to prepare the way for the entire and definite separation of the Discalced Carmelites from the ancient branch of the Order."

The Mass rite

Below are mentioned the chief differences between the Carmelite and Roman *Ordo Missae*. As with the Dominicans, there are many slight ceremonial differences but it would be tedious to list them all here.

At the *Asperges* the antiphon from Septuagesima until Easter is *Sancte Deus*; this is found in the original Holy Sepulchre rite. The celebrant on his way to the altar says Ps. 42 *submissa voce*. On arrival there, if it is a low Mass, he pours wine and water into the chalice and, having opened the Missal, goes to the foot of the altar for the preparatory prayers. They consist of versicle and response (V. *Confitemini Domino quoniam bonus*. R. *Quoniam in saeculum misericordia ejus*) the *Confiteor* (a shorter form than the Roman), *Misereatur* and *Indulgentiam* (differing only slightly from the Dominican form). On great feasts the introit anthem is recited three times as in some other rites previously mentioned. At high Mass the chalice is prepared between Epistle and Gospel.

At the offertory, on removing the chalice veil, the celebrant blesses the *oblata* saying *In nomine Patris*, etc. Chalice and paten are then offered together with the prayer *Suscipe sancta Trinitas*:

Accept, O holy Trinity, this offering which we make to you in memory of the passion, resurrection and ascension into heaven of our Lord Jesus Christ; and in honour of the blessed and glorious Mother of God, the ever Virgin Mary; and of all the saints who have been pleasing to you since the beginning of the world; may it avail to their honour and to our salvation to all interceding for us in heaven, may it be for the salvation of the living and the repose of the departed.

The *oblata* are then blessed. After the *Lavabo* the celebrant says the prayer, *In spiritu humilitatis.*

There are additional proper prefaces for St Elias, St Teresa, St John of the Cross and our Lady of Mount Carmel. After the consecration the celebrant says the prayer *Unde et memores* with arms outstretched in the form of a cross. The prayers before communion differ slightly from those in the Roman rite. Immediately after the blessing the *Salve Regina* is said.

The Carmelites celebrate the feasts of the canonized saints of their Order, but it is a pity that several are put down as O.N. (*Ordinis nostri*, "of our Order") in the calendar without historical grounds for the statement. St Euphrasia, St Telesphorus and St Spiridion, for example, were added to the Carmelite calendar in the sixteenth century by men who, believing that the Carmelite Order was founded in Old Testament times, reasoned that any saint of a certain antiquity must have belonged to it. The radical revision of the calendars of dioceses and religious Orders now in progress will no doubt deal with this relic of an uncritical age.

THE DOMINICAN RITE

Of all the variants of the Roman rite that of the Dominicans is probably the most widespread at the present day; in the past it exerted no inconsiderable influence on the liturgical observances of other Orders and some dioceses; it was even translated into Armenian. The character of the rite, its simplicity, its austerity, the absence of many of the special features that make some of the local rites which have now perished unattractive with their additions and seemingly tedious repetitions, render the Dominican liturgy especially apt for its purpose, the rite of men who, while not abandoning the solemn celebration of the daily liturgy, devote their lives to preaching and teaching.

St Dominic before founding his Order was a Canon Regular and the Dominicans have always preserved something of the canonical way of life, unlike the Franciscans whose emphasis seems to have lain elsewhere. St Dominic's insistence that the Office would be said *breviter et succincte* was enlarged upon by the reviser of the Dominican liturgy, Humbert de Romans, who laid down that the public worship of the friars should display a certain brevity lest recollection be destroyed, for long ceremonies would either hinder study or cause fatigue to the brethren. In fact Bruno of Olmütz complains in 1274 of the liturgical practices of the friars and the shortness of their Masses and says that as a consequence people prefer these Masses to the detriment of the monastic and parish churches.

Origins and history

Because the details of the Dominican *Ordo Missae* were said to resemble those of Paris it has often been stated that the Dominicans took their rite from that Church. The fact is that both evolved from a common source, the Franco-Roman Mass order. Of the special Parisian features, local developments not found in Rome, there is hardly any trace in the Dominican books. What have been regarded as Parisian elements are merely practices that were common all over France at the period.

The Dominican rite evolved by stages and its sources and origin can best be studied by a simple recapitulation of these stages. The need for a uniform liturgy was felt soon after the first Dominicans who had worked with Dominic at Toulouse (where they would have used the local rite) separated and were scattered in various parts of Europe. The adoption of the local rite wherever they went answered well enough until they met together again in chapter. Then the need for uniformity arose and an attempt at a uniform liturgy seems to have been made soon after Dominic's death (1221) but the haste with which it was put together militated against its proving satisfactory. Humbert de Romans, the fifth Master General, sums up the situation clearly: "At the beginning of the Order there was great variety in the Office and so an Office was compiled so that there might be uniformity. In time a commission of four of the brethren from four provinces was set up to revise and improve it. They did this and their arrangement was confirmed. But, as there were several points needing correction, Master Humbert was entrusted with a further revision which was approved by three chapters. And it is this last Office that is mentioned by the constitutions."

It was the chapter of 1245 which entrusted the commission of four friars of different nationalities with the task. Their work was approved by the general chapters of 1246, 1247 and 1248. Nevertheless, complaint was made of this recension of the Dominican liturgy and the chapter of 1254, which elected Humbert Master General, entrusted him with the work of final revision. His work was approved by the chapter of 1256 and by Clement IV in 1287.

That the work of the four friars, although it was confirmed by the chapter, should raise great opposition and that there was objection by some to Humbert's final revision poses a problem. Fr W. R. Bonniwell, O.P., in his important work on the Dominican rite,[38] suggests that the opposition came from the influential priory of St Jacques in Paris because the first Dominican Missal had been largely Parisian in inspiration and that of the four friars and Humbert was a Romanization. In fifteen years, he points out, the Dominicans "had changed from a Paris Missal to a Roman Missal. Here then, appar-

[38] *A History of the Dominican Liturgy* (New York, 1945), p. 192.

ently, we have the answer: the Dominican liturgists (of whom
Humbert de Romans was one) were fighting to Romanize
more fully the Dominican rite. Hence the battle." And here,
too, we have the answer to the supposed Parisian origin of the
Dominican rite.

The Dominican liturgy in the course of the Middle Ages
developed in much the same way as the other medieval rites.
Constant additions to the calendar upset the balance of temporal and sanctoral and as time went on revision of the text
became necessary. The rite was influenced to some extent by
the revision of the Roman rite by St Pius V. The recent reforms of the Roman rite, 1911, 1956 and 1960 have all been
adopted by the Dominicans though the essentials of the rite
have been preserved.

Mass rite

The *Asperges* before the Sunday conventual Mass contains
several variants not to be found in the Roman Missal. At low
Mass the chalice is prepared at the altar before Mass begins.
At high Mass the celebrant and ministers enter during the
second half of the introit chant (the introit is termed *officium*
in the Dominican Missal) the deacon carrying the Missal and
the subdeacon the book of Gospels. The prayers at the foot of
the altar are short: a versicle and response (*Confitemini
Domino quoniam bonus; Quoniam in saeculum misericordia
ejus*) are followed immediately by the *Confiteor.*[29] There is no
incense at the introit. After the collect at a high Mass the celebrant and ministers sit at the sedilia and the chalice is prepared there by the subdeacon who then takes the vessels to the
altar. At the singing of the Gospel in addition to candles and
incense the cross is carried.

[29] It is in this form: *Confiteor Deo omnipotenti et beatae Mariae
semper Virgini et beato Dominico patri nostro et omnibus sanctis et
vobis fratres quia peccavi nimis cogitatione, locutione, opere et omissione, mea culpa; precor vos orare pro me.* The *Misereatur* formula
is proper to the rite.

At the offertory host and chalice are offered together with the prayer *Suscipe sancta Trinitas* ("Accept, O holy Trinity, this offering which I make to you in memory of the passion of our Lord Jesus Christ and grant that it may ascend as pleasing to you and effect my salvation and that of all the faithful"). At the *Lavabo* only three verses of the psalm are said; this is followed by *In spiritu humilitatis* (a slight variation from the Roman form) said at the middle of the altar. There is no answer to the *Orate fratres*.

There is a proper preface for St Dominic and the new prefaces (St Joseph, the Dead, etc.) have been added from the Roman Missal. The canon is textually that of the Roman Missal but some of the rubrics differ. The celebrant is directed to extend his arms in the form of a cross at *Unde et memores*. At the commixture the prayer differs from the Roman form (it is *Haec sacrosancta commixtio* much as with the Carmelites and in some other medieval rites). The single prayer before the communion is *Domine Jesu Christe, Fili Dei vivi* and there is no *Domine non sum dignus*. There is a singular formula for the priest's communion (*Corpus et sanguis . . .*).

This short summary of the Dominican Mass rite will have sufficed to show its similarity with (and its differences from) the other Mass rites of about the same date. In general, the ceremonial differences from the modern Roman rite are in the direction of greater simplicity.

THE NEO-GALLICAN
LITURGIES

It has emerged very clearly in the course of the preceding pages that before the Council of Trent almost every ecclesiastical province in the West enjoyed its own variant of the Roman rite: the basis of these variants was Roman, of course, but many elements had been taken over from Gallican and other sources. By the sixteenth century it was obvious that a reform was necessary—a reform both of rubrics and of text for the one had in course of time grown exceedingly complex and the other, on account of the mistakes of copyists and the gradual insertion of spurious matter, was hopelessly corrupt. As we have seen, the reform of the liturgy required by the Council of Trent was completed under St Pius V with the publication of the Breviary (1568) and Missal (1570), but this reform left intact all the local variations (including those which have survived until this day and are mentioned in this book) which could show a prescription of at least two hundred years.

In 1570 two courses were open to those possessing, legitimately, local variations of the Roman rite. They could adopt the new Roman Missal, thus abandoning their own liturgical customs, or they could carry out the reform of their own books on the lines of what had already been done in the Roman rite. In France some dioceses adopted the Roman Missal and a printing of the reformed Roman books was ordered by the General Assembly of the Clergy of France in 1605; others reprinted their own books, taking the opportunity at the same time to carry out certain reforms. All this was legitimate enough and in the true tradition of liturgical development. It was only in the last part of the seventeenth century that the movement of what has been called "liturgical deviation" began to emerge and eventually to lead, by the time of the Vatican Council (1870), to the adoption of the Roman rite throughout France.

Liturgy is necessarily an expression of the religious mentality of a period and it has to be borne in mind that the latter part of the sixteenth and the first half of the seventeenth century in France witnessed a wonderful spiritual revival and that it was only when this revival suffered the setback provoked by Quietism and Jansenism that the "liturgical deviation" occurred. This period of liturgical history has been painted in exceedingly black colours by the liturgical polemical writers of the nineteenth century—by Dom Guéranger particularly—but it must be remembered that their campaign for the return to the Roman liturgy in the nineteenth century depended on their ability to show the illegitimacy of the local liturgies and in the heat of controversy much was written that will not bear detailed examination.

It is unnecessary here to go into the full details of the development, progress and final eclipse of the neo-Gallican liturgies. Certain landmarks can be pointed out, however. The first to retain our attention is the reformed Missal of Paris which was published in 1684 under de Harlay, archbishop at that time. Once more we find advanced the principle (already encountered in the history of the liturgy of Lyons and in that of the Carthusians) of the exclusion from the prayer of the Church (save in the Breviary lessons: the exception was made to include the lessons of the Fathers) of all that was not taken from Scripture. Thus introits like *Gaudeamus omnes in*

Domino (All Saints and other feasts), *Salve, sancta Parens* (Saturday Mass of our Lady) and others were replaced by biblical texts. Of its nature the principle is sound enough and was invoked, no doubt, in reaction against much of the unbecoming matter to be found in the medieval Missals; on the other hand, it requires to be said that the result in some of the French Missals of the eighteenth century was to produce an effect of intolerable pedantry.

The controversy over the "silent" recitation of the canon of the Mass forms a further stage in this story. The well-known Missal of Meaux (the diocese of Bossuet), published in 1709, inserted a red ℟. before the Amen at certain points in the canon to show that the congregation should make the response and, as a consequence, that the canon should be said aloud. But the most picturesque figure of all in this gallery of liturgical reform was Abbé Jubé, the parish priest of Asnières, near Paris. He insisted, says Fr Bouyer,

first of all on the public and collective character of the Mass. As a consequence, he never used the high altar in his church except on Sundays and feastdays when the congregation gathered together. He also restored the old Roman usage (which had endured longer in France than in Rome itself) of placing the linen cloth on the altar only just before Mass, and having no other cross or lights on the altar than the processional cross and tapers, which were set in place at the beginning of Mass. Jubé began Mass by saying the psalm *Judica* and the *Confiteor* along with the people; then he sat down at the Epistle side of the altar and listened to the Epistle and Gospel as they were sung by the assistant ministers, after having sung the collect himself. He sang the *Kyrie, Gloria* and *Credo* along with the people, instead of saying them in a low voice by himself. He also restored the offertory procession (which had never entirely disappeared from French churches) and had offerings of all kinds made in this procession which he later blessed at the *Per quem haec omnia* at the end of the canon, according to the original practice. He never began the canon before the Sanctus had been sung in full, and he said the prayers of the canon loudly enough to be heard by the whole congregation in his small church. In other words, he wanted once more to make the readings, the singing, the prayers, the offertory real, rather than merely conventional acts; and he wanted to have the sacrifice offered with the full, though always hierarchically ordered, participation of the Christian people. Dom Guéranger later regarded all these practices of Jubé as so many reasons for horror and dismay. But we of today can see in most of them intelligent and healthy improvements, had they been introduced with the consent of proper authority.[1]

In fact, many of these practices have been revived by recent liturgical reforms; Jubé's mistake was the one of acting on his own and without authority. Much the same can be said of the innovations in this field by Scipione Ricci at the famous Synod of Pistoia which was condemned by Pius VI (Bull *Auctorem Fidei*).

Many of the practices of these and other self-appointed liturgical reformers were in fact excellent in themselves, as we are now beginning to see, but enjoyed for many years a doubtful reputation acquired by their association with Jansenism— though it is perhaps well to remember that not everyone who was dubbed a Jansenist by the controversialists of the nineteenth century fully deserved the epithet.

In France the eighteenth century saw, then, diocese vying with diocese in the matter of bringing out a new Missal. By the time of the Revolution there were only twelve dioceses in France which followed the Roman rite—the rest all possessed reformed liturgies of one sort or another, all differing in many respects, all vitiated by the fact of the lack of authority for their compilation. The dioceses which thus endowed themselves with new Missals had all previously been in possession of legitimate Missals, variants of the Roman rite; by their unauthorized reform of their own rites they lost the benefit of the prescription of two hundred years' use granted by Pius V.

[1] Louis Bouyer, of the Oratory, *Liturgical Piety*, pp. 53–4.

The practical difficulties caused by this sort of thing became apparent when in 1809 the Concordat rearranged the boundaries of dioceses, suppressing some, joining others together. As a result liturgical differences were no longer confined to dioceses; now parishes in the same diocese found themselves in possession of differing liturgies and it was by no means rare to find three or four liturgies followed by the priests of the same diocese.

Such a state of affairs could not continue and under the leadership of Dom Guéranger, the founder of the Solesmes Congregation of Benedictines, a reaction in favour of the Roman rite occurred, not indeed without a certain heat of controversy; indeed as with all reactions it went too far and many of the liturgical traditions of the Churches of France were irretrievably lost. It is a pity that some of them did not do as Lyons did and retain some of their former—and legitimate— liturgical heritage, but a sober appraisal of the temper prevailing at the time reveals the great unlikelihood of that happening. In general, it was a period of liturgical ignorance when, through disregard of the necessary source material and the great respect paid to everything medieval, ideas about the Church's worship were coloured almost entirely by the prevailing romantic approach to history. In addition, the leaders of the movement back to the Roman liturgy were too near and far too affected by the events of the French Revolution and the controversies of the eighteenth century to be in a position to take a balanced view.[2]

[2] The implied criticism of Dom Guéranger in all this requires to be offset by the real contribution which he made to the liturgical revival. For this, see the volume in this series dealing with the history and principles of the liturgical movement.

THE SARUM RITE

This short appendix on the Sarum rite has been added because it was the best-known rite in the British Isles before the Reformation. It was used in the south of England far beyond the confines of the diocese of Salisbury to which it belonged and spread thence over much of Scotland and Ireland. Other similar liturgies were those of Hereford and Bangor. The Sarum rite was a medieval variant of the Roman rite with its origins probably in northern France. The usually quoted tradition is that St Osmund († 1099), a Norman nobleman who came over to England with William the Conqueror in 1066 and was appointed bishop of Sarum (or Salisbury) as a reward for his collaboration in the compilation of the Domesday Book, not only organized the chapter and built the first cathedral, but also compiled the service books for use in it, borrowing for the purpose many northern French customs. It seems more likely that the definitive Sarum rite was compiled by Richard le Poore († 1237; bishop 1217–28) who also founded the new cathedral.

The Sarum rite was a twelfth-century and early thirteenth-century recension of the Roman rite with an admixture of other, principally northern French customs. The development of the Roman rite, culminating in the revision of the Roman books following the Franciscan recension of the liturgy, is of slightly later date than the compilation of the Sarum books with the result that liturgies such as those of the Dominicans or Carmelites reveal greater affinities with the Sarum rite than with the Roman rite of St Pius V. This, it will be seen, appears quite clearly in the following summary description of the Sarum Mass rite.

The prayers at the foot of the altar were in the short form that we have already observed in the Carmelite and Dominican rites (cf. also Lyons and Braga), but the celebrant was enjoined to say the psalm (42) *Judica me* in the sacristy. The prayer *Aufer a nobis* was said but not *Oramus te*, in place of which the celebrant bowed low and made the sign of the cross. The introit (known here again as *Officium*) was repeated both before and after the *Gloria Patri*. The chalice was prepared between the Epistle and Gospel during the singing of the gradual. As in most of the medieval Missals lengthy and frequently undignified sequences were appointed for most occasions; few of them are of any great beauty.

The offertory prayers—simultaneous offering of host and chalice, *In spiritu humilitatis* after *Lavabo, Orate fratres et sorores* without answer—are very similar to present Dominican usage. The rest of the Mass differed only slightly from the modern Roman rite. Certain peculiarities may be noticed, however: the celebrant stretched out his arms in the form of a cross during the canon unless he had some manual act to perform, the prayers before the celebrant's communion differed and there was no blessing or last Gospel.

The principal difference between the Sarum rite and the modern Roman rite lay in the former's exuberance of ceremonial; in this it resembled many of the diocesan rites of France, especially of northern France. In the parish churches, no doubt, it was sober enough through want of the requisite ministers, but in the cathedral and collegiate churches the elaborate directions of the Sarum customary show it to have been extremely complicated, requiring a considerable number of persons for its due performance: three, five or seven subdeacons, a corresponding number of acolytes and so on.

"Rulers" of the choir (*rectores chori*) vested in copes, varied in number according to the solemnity celebrated.

The calendar was the basic Roman calendar with local variations of which there were a great number. The Sundays after Pentecost were counted after Trinity, thus the second Sunday after Pentecost in the Sarum rite was the first Sunday after Trinity with a corresponding displacement of collect, Epistle and Gospel. The colour sequence only took shape gradually. Its chief difference from present usage lay in the use of yellow for confessors. Red was the colour for Passiontide and plain linen ("ash" coloured) vestments were required for Lent.

The Sarum rite was used by the missionary priests in England after the break with Rome in the sixteenth century and continued in use until the publication of the Roman books; at the English College at Douai the Sarum Missal was in use until 1576 when the change to the Roman Missal was made. At the end of the nineteenth century when Westminster Cathedral was founded there was a proposal to revive the Sarum rite for use in the new foundation. Fortunately this idea was not pursued for a revival of this kind would have displayed an archaeological preoccupation entirely out of keeping with the character of Christian public worship. The Sarum rite was the expression of a particular religious mentality at a particular period; we have travelled too far since the Middle Ages to be able to adopt *en bloc* their liturgical practices, a point that is becoming clearer year by year as the reform of the Roman rite proceeds.

APPENDIX III

THE ROMAN-SLAVONIC
LITURGY

Properly speaking the Roman-Slavonic liturgy, as it is
called, is not a variant of the Roman rite at all. It is the
modern Roman rite as it is now used throughout the West,
but with Church Slavonic as its language instead of Latin. The
other name for it is the Glagolitic liturgy, because its liturgical
books are written in the Glagolitic alphabet known as Glagolica.

Fr Stephen Smrzik writes:

> The term Glagolica is derived from the Slavonic *glagol*,
> which means word, and *glagolat* which means to *speak, utter,
> say*.... In modern use among the Croats who follow the
> Roman-Slavonic rite *glagolat* means to celebrate the Roman-
> Slavonic rite. Glagolitic, therefore, is primarily the name of
> the alphabet, and not of the language or liturgy. In medieval
> times this alphabet was used in Croatia not only in the liturgy
> but also in all literary works and in all official business. When
> this alphabet later disappeared from use in public life it never-
> theless remained for several centuries incorporated in the
> liturgical books of the Roman-Slavonic rite. Because the
> Glagolica was during these centuries so closely linked with
> the Roman-Slavonic rite, forming its essential characteristic,
> the term Glagolitic rite became equated with the designation
> Roman-Slavonic rite.[1]

[1] Stephen Smrzik, S.J.: *The Glagolitic or Roman-Slavonic Liturgy*
(Cleveland, Ohio), 1959, page 15. See Select Bibliography.

There has been a good deal of discussion about the origin of the Glagolica. Traditionally it is traced back to St Cyril who evangelized Moravia and obtained from Adrian II permission to use Slavonic in the worship of the Church. Again, according to this tradition, St Cyril devised two alphabets, the Cyrillic and the Glagolitic, the former being used for the Byzantine rite and the latter for the Roman. For some centuries it was supposed that St Jerome invented the Glagolitic alphabet, but this theory was abandoned after J. Dobrovsky had pointed out that St Jerome had died some centuries before the Slavs settled in Dalmatia. It is generally accepted nowadays by Slavonic scholars that the Glagolica is older than the Cyrillica and that St Cyril invented the former and not the latter.[2]

The basis for St Cyril's invention has been much discussed, suggestions being put forward that the Glagolica was devised on the basis of Greek minuscula, Greek cursive script, Hebrew or Samaritan script. It is nowadays thought more likely that St Cyril's base was a Greek artificial script, the so-called cryptographia, used in specialized books.

> Since Greek cryptographic symbols, like those used today in mathematics, chemistry and other sciences, were known only to specialists, it is assumed that the Glagolica derived from them is an artificial script and quite complicated. That is why the Glagolica gradually declined after the death of both holy brothers (SS. Cyril and Methodius) and the newer Cyrillic alphabet began to flourish. It then spread everywhere among the Slavs of the Byzantine rite.[3]

In time the Glagolica became the national script in Croatia, developing steadily from the eleventh to the sixteenth centuries; the liturgical books, public documents and literary works were written in it.

The history of the Roman-Slavonic liturgy goes back, then, to St Cyril who translated the Roman Mass into Slavonic

[2] Smrzik, *op. cit.,* p. 17.
[3] Smrzik, *op. cit.,* pp. 18–19.

before his death in Rome in 869.[4] His companion St Methodius encountered difficulties on his return to Moravia and the
new pope, John VIII (872–82) forbade the liturgical use of
Slavonic. St Gregory VII (1243–54) renewed the prohibition
but Innocent IV (1243–54) authorized the use of Slavonic for
those places where it was still in use. The territory to which
this applied included Croatia with all the lands where the
Roman-Slavonic liturgy had come into use, that is, Istria,
Croatia, properly speaking, Dalmatia, Bosnia and Slavonia.[5]

The fourteenth to the sixteenth centuries were the golden
age of the Roman-Glagolitic liturgy; a decline began in the
seventeenth century caused by the shortage of liturgical books
printed in the Glagolitic script and, in addition, by the de-
creasing knowledge of the script and the language among the
clergy. In fact, the shortage of books caused priests to resort
to the use of these in Latin with the result, of course, that
knowledge of the language and script decreased still further.
This is clearly shown, for example, by the history of the
Glagolitic edition of the Roman Breviary. Editions of it were
printed in 1648, 1688 and a final edition in 1791.[6] This last has
become a rare book, a bibliographical treasure, and the clergy
today say their Office from a Latin Breviary; only the religious
of the Third Order Regular of St Francis have retained the use
of the Glagolitic Breviary, using the older editions.

In the case of the Missal the clergy were unable to abandon
so easily the liturgical traditions of their regions because their
people were too strongly attached to the use of Church
Slavonic. In consequence when a shortage of Glagolitic Missals occurred a hybrid liturgy was evolved.

[4] Whether he did this translation from the Gregorian sacramentary
or from the Greek of the so-called liturgy of St Peter (a Greek version
of the Roman rite in use in eastern Illyricum) need not concern us
here. The question is discussed at length in Smrzik, *op. cit.,* pp. 74–95.

[5] See Angelus A. de Marco, O.F.M.: *Rome and the Vernacular*
(Westminster, Md., 1961), p. 46.

[6] *Breviarium Romanum Slavonico idiomate iussu SS. D.N. Papae
Pii VI editum in duas anni partes divisum.* Romae, 1791.

The priests executed the singing and in general all the vocal portions of the Mass either from memory or from old Slavonic handbooks and the people answered in the same language. But the canon and other silent parts of the Mass were read from a Missal written in the Latin language. Of course, in singing either from memory or from old handbooks, the priests tended to introduce some innovations more or less close to modern Croatian.[7]

Editions of the Missal were printed in 1483, 1631 and 1741. The shortage of liturgical books and the consequent prevalence of *schiavetto* saw the Roman-Slavonic liturgy reduced to its lowest ebb. A revival occurred with the pontificate of Leo XIII. A new edition of the Glagolitic Missal, revised in accordance with the oldest manuscripts of the Croatian recension, appeared in 1893 (a reprint was made in 1905).

This was the last edition of the Missal in Glagolitic script. Knowledge of the script had so far declined during the twentieth century that after the First World War the bishops of Yugoslavia "requested a transliteration of the Missal into the Latin alphabet. In addition, with the introduction of the Latin script, the bishops aimed at a greater diffusion of the Roman-Slavonic liturgy in their country. The Holy See granted the necessary permission. . . . This Missal was issued in Rome in 1927."[8]

The present position of the use of the Roman-Slavonic liturgy is as follows. It is the liturgy of about one million Catholics in Croatia in the dioceses of Porec-Pula, Rijeka, Senj, Krk, Zadar, Sibernik, Hvar (a few parishes only) and Split. In 1920 the use of the Glagolitic liturgy was allowed several times a year (on certain feasts) in some churches in Czechoslovakia. In 1925 permission was given for the liturgy to be used throughout Yugoslavia on the feast of SS. Cyril and Methodius (July 5th) and the concordat drawn up in 1935

[7] Smrzik, *op. cit.*, p. 22. This practice of a mixture of languages was known as *schiavetto*.
[8] Smrzik, *op. cit.*, p. 16.

made provision for the introduction of the Glagolitic liturgy throughout the country at the bishop's discretion. This concordat was not ratified in Belgrade so its concessions never came into force and until the end of the Second World War the position was governed by the decree of the papal Secretariate of State[9] issued in 1952 which permits the extension of the Roman-Slavonic liturgy in dioceses where it had previously been in use.

What has been said above applies only to the Missal. The Breviary, as we have seen, is said by the clergy in Latin and the Ritual offices are performed in modern Croatian, a concession dating back to 1930 in its present form, but already in the seventeenth century the Holy See had authorized in Croatia the use of the vernacular in the administration of the sacraments and a Croatian translation was published in 1640 in Rome which was adopted by all the Roman-Slavonic dioceses. That is why, Fr Smrzik points out, the Ritual has never been printed in Glagolitic characters.

[9] And not now by the decree of 1906 as de Marco states, *op. cit.*, p. 48. See Smrzik, *op. cit.*, p. 118.

SELECT BIBLIOGRAPHY

In this series: AMIOT, F.: *History of the Mass*; DALMAIS, I.-H., O.P.: *The Eastern Liturgies*; DENIS-BOULET, Noële M.: *The Christian Calendar.*

BAUMSTARK, Anton: *Comparative Liturgy,* revised by Bernard Botte, O.S.B., translated by F. L. Cross, London, Mowbray, and Westminster, Md, Newman Press, 1958.

BISHOP, Edmund: *Liturgica Historica, Papers on the Liturgy and Religious Life of the Western Church,* London and New York, Oxford Univ. Press, 1918.

BISHOP, W. C.: *The Mozarabic and Ambrosian Rites,* edited by C. L. Feltoe, London, Mowbray, and Milwaukee, Morehouse Publishing Co., 1924.

BONNIWELL, W. R., O.P.: *A History of the Dominican Liturgy,* New York, Benziger, 1945.

BOUYER, L.: *Liturgical Piety,* Notre Dame, Ind., Univ. of Notre Dame Press, 1954.

CABROL, Fernand, O.S.B.: *The Mass of the Western Rites,* London, Sands, 1934.

DUCHESNE, L.: *Christian Worship, its Origin and Evolution,* London, S.P.C.K., 1903.

FELTOE, C. L.: *Sacramentarium leonianum,* Cambridge and New York, Cambridge Univ. Press, 1906.

FRERE, W.: *The Principles of Religious Ceremonial,* London, Mowbray, 1928.

JUNGMANN, J. A., S.J.: *The Mass of the Roman Rite, its Origins and Development* (Missarum Solemnia), translated by F. A. Brunner, C.SS.R. Two volumes, New York, Benziger, 1951 and 1956.

KING, Archdale A.: *Liturgies of the Religious Orders,* London, Longmans, and Milwaukee, Bruce, 1955; *Liturgies of the Primatial Sees,* London, Longmans, 1957; *Liturgies of the Past,* London, Longmans, 1959.

MARCO, Angelus A. de, O.F.M.: *Rome and the Vernacular*, Westminster, Md, Newman Press, 1961.

SMRZIK, Stephen, S.J.: *The Glagolithic or Roman-Slavonic Liturgy*, Cleveland, Ohio, Slovak Institute, 1959.

VAN DIJK, S. J. P., O.F.M., and WALKER, J. Hazelden: *The Origins of the Modern Roman Liturgy*, London, Darton, Longman and Todd, and Westminster, Md, Newman Press, 1960.

WILSON, H. A.: *The Gelasian Sacramentary*, London and New York, Oxford Univ. Press, 1894; *The Gregorian Sacramentary*, London, Henry Bradshaw Society, 1915.

The Twentieth Century Encyclopedia of Catholicism

The number of each volume indicates its place in the over-all series and not the order of publication.

TWENTIETH CENTURY ENCYCLOPEDIA OF CATHOLICISM

All titles are subject to change.